BIJAPUR

THE

OLD CAPITAL OF THE ADIL SHAHI KINGS

BIJAPUR

THE
OLD CAPITAL OF THE ADIL SHAHI KINGS

A GUIDE TO ITS RUINS
WITH HISTORICAL OUTLINE

BY

HENRY COUSENS, M.R.A.S.

GYAN

Published by

Gyan Publishing House
5, Ansari Road
Daryaganj, New Delhi-110002
Phone: 011-47034999, 9811692060
E-mail: books@gyanbooks.com

Distribution Network
gyanbooks.com
India, USA, Canada, UK, Australia

ISBN: 978-93-6208-570-2 (HB)
First Published, 1889

2nd Impression 2024

Printed at: Gyan Press, Delhi.

BIJAPUR THE OLD CAPITAL OF THE ADIL SHAHI KINGS
Author: HENRY COUSENS

BIJAPUR

THE CAPITAL OF THE ADIL SHAHI KINGS.

BIJAPUR

THE OLD CAPITAL OF THE ADIL SHAHI KINGS.

A GUIDE TO ITS RUINS
WITH HISTORICAL OUTLINE

BY

HENRY COUSENS, M.R.A.S.

SUPERINTENDENT, ARCHÆLOGICAL SURVEY OF INDIA
WESTERN CIRCLE.

POONA:
SCOTTISH MISSION INDUSTRIES COMPANY, LIMITED.

1905.

PREFACE TO FIRST EDITION.

THERE has hitherto existed no work on Bijapur and its ruins that could be used as a guidebook. The portfolio of the late James Fergusson, LL.D., and Col. Meadows Taylor has long been out of print, and since it was written much fresh information has been gathered that would necessitate a revised edition. The best account that has been published is that by Mr. H. F. Silcock, C.S., for the Bijapur District volume of the Bombay Gazetteer, but the price and bulk of the book, of which the account of the city forms but a part, precludes its use as a handbook. The want of some guidebook to Bijapur has been much felt, especially by tourists and visitors. Mr. Ebden, the Collector of Bijapur, pointed this out to Government, and asked that Mr. Silcock should be requested, since he was willing to undertake it, to re-arrange his Gazetteer account in the form of a guide. After this correspondence I visited Bijapur and spent a whole season there surveying its buildings in the ordinary course of my official duties, so that I had special opportunities of becoming intimately acquainted with its monuments. It was my intention on proceeding to Bijapur to write a small handbook or guide to the city. I had not then heard of the arrangement with Mr. Silcock; but when the latter knew of my intention through Mr. Ebden, he, finding his time very much occupied with his own official work, suggested that I should take it in hand. Later, in a letter to Government, Dr. Burgess, the Director General of Archæological Surveys in India, also suggested that my notes, as then forwarded by him to Government, might form the foundation of such a guide-book as was necessary. The Government of Bombay Resolutions in connection with the matter are Nos. 1344 of 4th May 1887, 3873 of 23rd December 1887, and 4119 of 22nd November 1888. It is hoped the present little sketch will meet all the requirements of visitors. Drawings, photographs, and full notes have been made for a large work which will be published by Government in the series of volumes of the Archæological Survey of Western India, and in which, those who wish to study the architecture and history of Bijapur, will find abundant materials.

I have to thank Mr. E. J. Ebden, C. S., Collector of Bijapur, for much help while I was working there; and certain discoveries he made in his leisure hours during last monsoon have added materially to the stock of information. Mr. Reinold, late executive Engineer of Bijapur, kindly allowed me to copy a good map of the city which he had in his office, and which, with additions, is now presented with this book. Mr. A. S. MacDonald Ritchie, who was for some time at Bijapur as Assistant Engineer, also gave me much assistance; and his minute information respecting the buildings, in and around the city, saved me much time and trouble in hunting it up for myself. My thanks are due to him for this. The translation of the old Persian inscriptions by Mr. Rehatsek of Bombay has settled many doubtful points and added new facts.

I have consulted James Fergusson and Meadows Taylor's Work, Taylor's Indian History, Mr. Silcock's Gazetteer account, Scott's Ferishta, Grant Duff's History of the Marathas, Bernier, Baldæus, etc., but, more especially, for the Historical Outline, an old Persian manuscript history which I obtained at Bijapur, and which gives a very full and accurate account of the Ádil Shahis.

I have purposely avoided classing the buildings in groups in the description of them, for in reading the accounts of several mosques, or tombs, in succession, there would be much repetition. In the text diacritical marks have not been used.

The Itinerary (p. 101) will help visitors to arrange their tours round the town with the least loss of time. A scale of fares for public conveyances is appended, and will also be found useful.

Jalal-ud-din Bangi, a Muhammadan lad, who lives in Bijapur, knows the city and its ruins well, and will be found about the best guide available. He does not, however, know English.

The design impressed on the cover is from the large wrought iron screen that was dug up when excavations were made in the citadel. It is now framed and placed in the little station Church near the Gagan Mahal.

H. C.

Palitana, Feb. 1889.

NOTE:—The first edition has been revised and brought up to date. The lad Jalal-ud-din is a lad no longer, but he is quite as efficient a guide. The design on the cover is changed, the present disc being taken from the plaster ornament on the face of Ali Shahid Pir's mosque.

H. C.

Simla, August, 1906.

CONTENTS.

"I asked of Time for whom those temples rose,
That prostrate by his hand in silence lie;
His lips disdained the myst'ry to disclose,
And, borne on swifter wing, he hurried by!
'The broken columns whose?' I asked of Fame;
(Her kindling breath gives life to works sublime;)
With downcast looks of mingled grief and shame
She heaved the uncertain sigh and followed Time.
Wrapt in amazement o'er the mouldering pile,
I saw Oblivion pass with giant stride;
And while his visage wore Pride's scornful smile,
'Haply thou knowest, then tell me, whose' I cried,
'Whose these vast domes that e'en in ruin shine?'
'I reck not whose,' he said: 'they now are mine.'"

GUIDE TO BIJAPUR

OBJECTS OF INTEREST.

GENERAL Description of the City.—Bijapur, once the capital of the Dekhan, is situated, as the crow flies, two hundred and forty miles south-east of Bombay. It is reached by the Southern Maratha Railway, from its junction with the Great Indian Peninsula Railway at Hotgi, near Sholapur. The city is fifty-eight miles south of this junction. The journey from Hotgi is very uninteresting, the line traversing, for the most part, long stretches of dry, barren, stony soil, with little vegetation, save in the valleys of the Bhima and its tributaries which are crossed *en route*. At the fortieth mile from Hotgi, the line crosses a ridge, at the end of a range of low hills, from which high ground the first glimpse of Bijapur is obtained. Far away to the left, a small dark, square, object is seen, in bold relief, against the sky on the southern horizon. This is the great Gol Gumbaz, the tomb of Sultan Muhammad, the largest building in the Dekhan. It is a very conspicuous object for miles from the city on either side, and it has even been reported to have been seen from Bagalkot, fifty-six miles to the south, but this assertion needs to be taken *cum grano salis*. From this point, except for short intermissions, when the line descends into the intervening valleys, it remains in sight, first on one side, and then on the other, as the line changes its direction; and grows larger and larger, and more distinct, as the distance between is shortened. Gradually other large buildings rise into view, among them being the Jami Masjid, the Sat Manjli, the "Two Sisters," and the lofty gun tower of Haidar Khan, following each other along the horizon, in this order, to the west of the Gol Gumbaz. Then, further away still to the west, and on higher ground, beyond the city, stands the white tomb of Pir Amin, with the village of Dargapur clustered around it. To the east of the Great Dome, and conspicuous among lesser buildings and ruins which dot the bare looking country without the walls, are the unfinished tomb of Jahan Begam and that of Ain-ul-Mulk, with its well proportioned dome.

As the city is reached, it begins to unfold itself, and, when the high ground, just outside the walls to the north, is attained, a grand uninterrupted view of the whole town presents itself. Why such an exposed position for a city was selected, that had to defend itself against many enemies, it is difficult to conceive. There is nothing, whatever, in the natural features of the ground to give it any claim to preference as a suitable site. It was probably of gradual growth, and Yusaf Adil Khan found it already an important military station when he was sent there as its commandant and governor. It was, indeed, intended, at one time, to move the seat of government to Nauraspur, several miles to the west of Bijapur, and Ibrahim II. began to build palaces and fortifications with that object; but the ever officious astrologers stepped in, with their warnings, and the project was given up. The whole of the eastern quarter of Bijapur is completely overlooked and commanded by the higher ground, which surrounds, and is close up to, its walls. A few good batteries placed along on these ridges, would, in a very short time, lay the city in ruins; for the gunners, while themselves securely entrenched or hidden behind the crests, would have a clear view of every building, and of everything that might be going on within the walls. We can only suppose that, at the time Bijapur was selected as the head quarters of a province by the Bidar government, guns were little used, and that, for some time after they did come into use, they were such primitive weapons, and their practice was so bad, that the town was comparatively safe. When, however, Aurangzib came down upon it with superior artillery, and better served, the city soon lay at his mercy.

Bijapur has been called the Palmyra of the Dekhan. As with Palmyra, the traveller comes upon a city of ruins, across miles of barren country. It loses much, now, by its easy access, that Palmyra gains by the excitement and dangers of the road. Not many decades ago the likeness was greater. The way was not altogether safe from Maratha freebooters; and when the city was reached, it was found well nigh deserted, for few people lived within its walls. The character of the soil, and its scant productiveness, so far as may be seen on the journey down, and the arid stretches of dry land surrounding the city, cause one to wonder how so great a population, as Bijapur once contained, could have been fed. The secret lies not far off. A few miles to the south runs the river Don, the valley of which is so fertile that its fertility has passed into a proverb :—

> "If the harvest of the Don be good, who shall eat it?
> If bad, who will get anything to eat?"

This was, then, the main source of supply to the people of Bijapur. It was, however, supplemented by produce from the valleys of the Bhima and Krishna.

Meadows Taylor best describes the scene of desolation which met the traveller directly he entered the walls of Bijapur, not so many years ago. "But mournful as it is, the picturesque beauty of the combinations of the buildings, the fine old tamarind and peepul trees, the hoary ruins, and distant views of the more perfect edifices, combine to produce an ever-changing and impressive series of landscapes. Nowhere in the Deccan, not even at Beedar, at Goolburgah, or in the old fort of Golcondah, is there any evidence of general public taste and expenditure, like that proved by the remains in Beejapoor—and for days together the traveller, or sketcher, will wander among these remains with his wonder still excited and unsatisfied. It is not by the grandeur of the edifices now perfect, noble as they are,. that the imagination is so much filled, as by the countless other objects of interest in ruin, which far exceed them in number. Palaces, arches, tombs, cisterns, gateways, minarets, all carved from the rich brown basalt rock of the locality, garlanded by creepers, broken and disjointed by peepul, or banian trees, each, in its turn, is a gem of art, and the whole a treasury to the sketcher or artist. . . . . The interior of the citadel is almost indescribable, being nearly covered with masses of enormus ruins, now almost shapeless, interspersed with buildings still perfect. All those which had vaulted roofs are sound, but all in which wood existed are roofless and irreparably ruined . . . . In the citadel the visitor, if he be acquainted with its past history, will have many a scene of historical interest shown to him. The court which the devoted Dilshad Agha, and her royal mistress Booboojee Khanum, Queen of Yusuf Adil Shah, clad in armour, and fighting among their soldiers, defended against the attempts of the treacherous Kumal Khan to murder the young king Ismail; the place where the son of Kumal Khan stood, when the young king pushed over a stone from the parapet above, which crushed him to death; the window where the dead body of Kumal Khan was set out, as if alive, to encourage the soldiery in their brutal assault: the place on the ramparts where Dilshad Agha threw over the ropes, and the faithful bands of Persians and Moghuls ascended by them and saved the Queen and her son. All these will be pointed out with every accompanying evidence of probability and truth; as well as the apartment whence the traitor Kishwar Khan dragged the noble hearted Queen Chand Beebee to her prison at Sattara. Then in a lighter vein, the visitor will be told of the merry Monarch Mahmood ; he will be shown the still entire and exquisitely proportioned and ornamented room where happy hours were passed with the beautiful Rhumba ; and though it was much defaced when the Rajah of Sattara began with his own dagger to scrape the gilding from the walls, there are still traces of the picture of the jovial king and his lovely mistress. Such, and hundreds of other tales of wild romance and reality which linger amidst these royal precincts, will, if the visitor choose to listen to them, be told him by descendants of those who took part in them, with as fond and vivid a remembrance as the Moorish legends of the Alhambra are told there.

"For such legends of that beautiful memorial of past greatness, an interest for all time has been created ; but no one has succeeded in awakening for Bijapur any corresponding feeling, and far grander as its memorials are, accounts of them are listened to with a cold scepticism or indifference which hitherto nothing has aroused. And yet, inspired by the effect of these beautiful ruins with the glory of an Indian sun lighting up palace and mosque, prison and zenana, embattled tower and rampart, with a splendour which can only be felt by personal experience, it may be hoped that some eloquent and poetic pen may be found to gather up the fleeting memorials of traditions which are fast passing away, and invest them with a classic interest which will be imperishable. Above all, however, these noble monuments may serve to lead our countrymen to appreciate the intellect, the taste, and the high power of art and execution which they evince, to consider their authors not as barbarians, but in the position to which their works justly entitled them; and to follow, in the history of those who conceived them, that Divine scheme of civilization and improvement, which, so strangely and so impressively, has been confided to the English nation."

Since the above was written a great change has come over the city—a change that is still going on, and will continue to do so, until, in a few years hence, those who return to it, after an absence of twelve or fifteen years, will hardly recognise it. Of the wisdom of this change it must be left to individuals to judge for themselves. Some, basing their opinions upon utility, will welcome the improvements, others will deplore the too free hand of the utilitarian. The former will, no doubt, commend the policy which puts to use all that can be used, and looks upon any other idea as pure maudlin sentiment; whereas the latter will ever regret that old associations, traditional and historical, and their objects, have, under the guise of modern improvement, been irretrievably separated: that the objects they look upon are not those of the past; that the hoary old ruins, clad in picturesque attire, garnished by nature with many a festoon and wreath of creepers, are being stripped of the mantle nature has woven for them, and are either exposed to view in naked ugliness, or are cleared away entirely by the hands of convicts. But a reaction has set in. Government has interested itself in the welfare and preservation of these grand old memorials of a past kingdom's greatness, and, although what has been done cannot be undone, we shall now see all, that has withstood the ravages of time and man, well cared for. At present, although the citadel is completely altered from what it was thirty years ago, the rest of the town still preserves some of its old aspect. The greater part of it is waste land, strewn with the foundations and ruins of houses which once occupied almost every yard of it. The old roads and streets, between the heaps of ruins of fallen walls, can, in many instances, be clearly traced. Prickly-pear tries to hold possession of every patch of waste ground, and jealously encompasses and guards the crumbling ruins. It had so overrun the place, that the local authorities found it no easy task to make clearances in it, for wherever it was thrown or buried it soon asserted itself again, and started up a fresh crop, unless it was dried and burnt. Considerable areas, within the walls, are cultivated fields. The present population has spread itself across the west end of the city and down about the Jami Masjid, and a few hamlets are scattered about among its ruins. The largest suburb is that of Shahapur, without the north-western gate.

The Walls.—The city is surrounded by a fortified wall, consisting of ninety-six bastions, with their connecting curtain walls, and five principal gates, with their flanking bastions.

The walls have been well built of stone and mortar, backed up with a good breadth of rammed earth between the outer and inner casings. Along the top of this is a broad platform, running from bastion to bastion and over the gates; and this is protected by a high battlemented wall, which rises from the top of the curtain wall. The bastions, which are placed at most regular intervals, are generally semi-circular in plan, sometimes polygonal, but nowhere square. Upon these, guns were mounted, and gun platforms were constructed for them. These are curious and well worth examination. In the centre of the paved platform is a small circular hole, for the pivot upon which the carriage revolved, and at a distance from it, decided by the length of gun to be mounted, are two opposite segments of a channelled ring, in which the wheels of the carriage travelled as the gun was swung round. Connecting the ends of these two segments, towards the back of the gun, is a segmental recoil wall, built back at such a distance that the cascable of the gun very nearly touches it. When firing, this small space, betwen the two, was probably wedged up firmly in order to counteract the recoil of the gun, and prevent undue strain upon the pivot. It appears that, in the original construction of these bastions, no cover was provided for the gunners; but it has been subsequently added to some, if not all, by building a low shelter wall round the crest of the bastions, leaving embrasures, at intervals, big enough to fire through. Where these shelter walls exist, they are very light and flimsy, and could only have afforded protection against musket balls ; shot from cannon would have knocked them to pieces very quickly. The Feringhi Burj, unlike the rest, has been built to accommodate several small pieces of cannon, one before each embrasure, mounted upon blocks of masonry, and each provided with a kind of universal joint, so that it might be quickly turned about and pointed in any direction. Outside the walls, and running nearly the whole length round them, is a deep broad moat, and, beyond this, can still be traced remains of a covert way.

The Gates.—The principal gates are five—the Makka gate on the west, the Shahapur gate at the north-west corner, the Bahmani gate on the north, the Allahpur gate on the east, and the Fateh gate on the south-east. They are well protected by flanking bastions, double gates, and covered approaches. The Fateh gate was originally known as the Mangoli gate, called after the town of that name, twelve miles distant, to which the road through it led. But when Aurangzib entered the city in triumph by it, he ordered that it should, thenceforth, be called the Fateh Darwaja or Gate of Victory. The Makka gate has, subsequently to its erection, been further strengthened and fortified, upon its inner side, and has been converted into a small stronghold, safe against enemies within or without. It is said to have been further added to by the Peshwa's government, probably as better protection for their small garrison and revenue offices. The British, on taking over Bijapur, also located their Government Offices in this place, until later conversions, of some of the old buildings of the citadel, provided them with better accommodation. It has been occupied by a school. It is a great pity that this fine old gate should not be opened out and used. It is the natural outlet, on the west, to the long road that traverses Bijapur from east to west; and which road now, just as it abuts upon the gateway, and seeks exit, is diverted at right-angles, and follows the wall four hundred yards further to the north, before it reaches the smaller Zohrahpur gate.

In addition to these five principal gates, there are several smaller ones, among which are the Zohrahpur gate, between the Makka and Shahapur gates, and the Padshahpur gate, now in disuse, on the east, near the railway station. There were also numerous *diddis*, or small posterns, leading out into the ditch.

The whole circuit of the walls measures about six and a quarter miles, and the whole area, within them, is about 1,300 acres or two and a half square miles.

The Arkillah* or Citadel walls, with a circuit of one and a tenth mile, were very similar in arrangement to the outer walls. More than half of these have been levelled and cleared away, but it is probable that there were three gates—one still existing on the south, one on the west near the Sat Manjli, and one on the north. There is another, which is still used on the east, opposite the Asar Mahal, but it is a postern. On this side, an arched viaduct connected the interior of the citadel with the Asar Mahal, just without its walls, and was

* Probably Arku'llah, or Ark Allah, the "Castle of Allah."

used when the Asar Mahal served its first and original purpose—a hall of justice.

The Waterworks.—The waterworks of Bijapur, like those of almost all old Muhammadan towns, were, in their day, perfect; abundance of pure wholesome water was brought into the city from two principal sources—one from Torweh, four miles to the west, and the other from the Begam talao to the south. These sources, being without the walls, could easily be cut off by an army investing the city; but this contingency was evidently foreseen and met by the plentiful distribution of tanks and wells within the walls, supplied from these sources, and which, when once filled, would render the besieged independent of the source for months together. Wherever the remains of Muhammadan buildings are met, this characteristic marks them all. They had a special fondness for the presence of water. They knew full well, and appreciated, the cooling effect of tanks and cisterns of cold water within and around their dwellings. These, together with cool chunam or marble pavements, covered in with thick masonry walls and roofs, afforded a luxurious retreat from the glare and scorching heat of a summer sun. In their palaces, even in cool subterranean vaults, they had their chunam-lined baths and fountains. In the Sat Manjli they had at least one basin or bath on each floor, with octagonal, square, or fluted sides; and, away upon the highest storey now remaining, are traces of a bath. Their palaces usually had a large square tank within the walled enclosure. It may be seen in the ruined palaces of Fateh Khan and Mustafa Khan. The reservoir of the latter was filled from a well close by, the water being drawn up by a *mot* into an elevated cistern, from which it ran to the tank through earthen pipes set in masonry. Traces of these may be seen from the well to the tank. When the tank was filled to the brim, the water was allowed to run off down shallow stone channels, in different directions, through the garden that surrounded it; and, to give a prettier effect to the running water, the floor of the channel was cut into zigzag ridges, against which the water struck and rebounded in thousands of little ripples. These ripple stones were, in many instances, of very much more complicated patterns. Lying about the Anand Mahal are several fragments of these. They are divided into large compartments, and each of these is channelled into the plan of a maze or labyrinth. The water entered at one end, and travelled through all these channels, in and out, redoubling on itself a dozen times; finally it flowed out at the opposite end into another, where it had to go through the same meanderings. The effect must have been exceedingly pretty, for the divisions between the channels are very narrow, just enough to separate the two streams of water, on either side, running in different directions. Then again, in some, the water is made to beat against innumerable little fishes, carved in all sorts of positions, in high relief, on the floor of the channel.

There is a curious little building, well worth an inspection, in the south east corner of the town, not far from the Jami Masjid, called Mubarak Khan's Mahal. It was built entirely for a display of waterworks. It was a three storeyed pavilion. The lower storey is square, the next octagonal, and the upper, a small one, supports the dome. Water was carried all through the building in pipes buried in the masonry. Around the plinth is a row of peacock brackets, which are channelled along their tops, and out through the mouths of the peacocks. Behind them, on the plinth, are two rows of pipes, which supplied them with water. Around the next storey was a cornice, some of the brackets of which were chanelled in the same manner, and in the dome are holes at intervals which are the outlets of small pipes. When the water was turned on, itspouted from all these brackets and the dome, and fell into a cistern, in the midst of which the pavilion stood. In the second storey was a small cistern, and, what appears to be the remains of a fountain, occupies the floor of the third. On the roof of the small building, beside this one, was a large shallow tank; and in the bottom of this, and let into the ceiling, is a large circular slab pierced with holes. This was intended as a shower bath. There are several of these buildings out at Kumatgi, about ten miles east of Bijapur, which will be described further on.

From the Torweh direction, the water was brought towards the city by a great subterranean tunnel. A curious thing about this tunnel is, that it is built up on one side only, the other side being the natural *murum* wall through which it is cut. The reason of this is that the strata of rock and *murum*, through which the tunnel passes, dips from south to north, so that the water, percolating down through the strata, falls into the tunnel and is caught, the masonry on the opposite side preventing its escape again. The stream is thus considerably increased by the addition it gains on its way to the city. It is vaulted over and its direction can be traced very easily by the masonry air shafts at regular intervals along its route.

From the Begam talao, on the south of the town, the water is brought in through earthern pipes. These pipes are in short lengths, being made with a shoulder, on one end of each length, into which the next pipe fits, the whole being then embedded in concrete. Along the line of these pipes, at intervals, are tall open water towers, built for the purpose of relieving the great pressure there would otherwise be in the pipes.

The principal tanks and wells in the town are the great Taj Bauri, the largest and most important; the Chand Bauri near the Shahapur gate; the Bari and Mubarak Khan's Bauris in the south-east; the Masa and Nim Bauris in the north-east quarter of the city; the Ilal and Nagar Bauris; and the Jami Masjid Bauri to the south of the Jami Masjid. There were many other large ones, the ruins of which may be seen, but they have been neglected, and now hold no water.

Bijapur Architecture.—Bijapur suddenly sprung into existence as an important factor in the affairs of Dekhan, rapidly attained the highest rank among its states, and just as suddenly collapsed. It enjoyed the dignity of a capital, the seat of the Adil Shahis, for two hundred years, and then surrendered its liberty to the overwhelming power of Dehli, and was thenceforth compelled to take the subordinate rank of one of its numerous dependencies.

It may be as well to insert here a list of the Kings of Bijapur, with their dates, and the names of the principal buildings ascribed to them.

YUSAF ADIL SHAH (1489—1510.)—The first enclosure of the citadel or "Ark"; the Dekhani Idgah; and Yusaf's old Jami mosque (Asen Beg's mosque).

ISMAIL ADIL SHAH (1510—1534.)—The Champa Mahal (1521).

MALLU ADIL SHAH, (1534, deposed.)—No works.

IBRAHIM (I.) ADIL SHAH (1534—1557.)—Mosque at Ibrahimpur (1526); the Sola Thami Mahal (1528); strengthened the fortifications of the citadel; the Ghalib Masjid; and the old Jami Mosque near the tomb of Hazrat Jaffar Sakkaf (1551).

ALI (I.) ADIL SHAH (1557—1580.)—His own tomb in the south west quarter of the city; the city walls and fortifications (1565); the Gagan Mahal (1561); the Chand Bauri; and the commencement of the great Jami Masjid (1537).

Also the fortifications of Shahdurg (1558); and part of the fortified walls of Raichor (1570).

IBRAHIM (II.) ADIL SHAH (1580—1626)—The mausoleum of Taj Sultana, called the Ibrahim Rauza (1626); Sat Manjli or Sat Khan-ka Mahal (1583); the Haidar Burj (1583);

Malika Jahan Masjid (1587); the Anand Mahal (1589); the Sangat or Nauras Mahal and other buildings at Nauraspur (1599 to 1624); and the Taj Bauri 1620).

MUHAMMAD ADIL SHAH (1626—1656.)—His own tomb, the great Gol Gumbaz; the Begam talao waterworks (1651); the decoration of the Jami Masjid *mehrab*; and the Asar Mahal.

ALI (II.) ADIL SHAH (1656—1672.)—The commencement of his own tomb, to the north of the citadel; and the rebuilding of a length of the city walls close beside the Landa Kasba bastion (1662.)

SIKANDAR ADIL SHAH (1672—1686). No works.

The real building period of Bijapur did not commence until Ali (I.) Adil Shah ascended the *masnad*. He was a great patron of the arts and welcomed artists and learned men to his capital. One of the first buildings undertaken was the Jami Mosque, which, for simplicity of design, impressive grandeur, and the solemn hush of its corridors, stands unrivalled. It is, too, the best proportioned building in the city. It was after Ali Adil Shah, laden with spoils, returned from the great battle of Talikot and the destruction of Vijayanagar, that the walls and fortifications of the city were taken in hand and completed. Portions were allotted to each of his generals, hence the various styles and degrees of finish of the different sections of the same. The Adaulat Mahal, the Sona Mahal, and the first attempts to bring water into the town, are ascribed to him.

Ibrahim II. followed up the good example of his father, and continued to adorn the city with some of its most ornate buildings. He raised the elaborate pile of the Ibrahim Rauza, the most picturesque group at Bijapur.

Muhammad, who succeeded him, has left us one of the greatest domes the world has seen, over his own tomb, the Gol Gumbaz.

Ali II., who followed, being determined to outdo them all, commenced his own mausoleum on so grand a scale that he had not time to complete it ere his death dispersed the workmen, and it remains a splendid ruin, a lasting monument to his ambition. With this tomb ended, virtually, the building age of Bijapur. It flourished from the laying of the foundation stone of the Jami Masjid, about 1537, to the death of Ali II. in 1672, a hundred and thirty five years.

In the Jami Masjid we have the style, which is so peculiar to Bijapur, coming upon us in its full development, in its purest and best form. It would appear that not only the style, but its architects, were imported, and that subsequent buildings were erected, upon the lines laid down by these men, by their descendents and local builders who copied them. It is a fact that no subsequent building is equal to this one for its perfect proportions. The art weakened, and a sign of this is the lavish and profuse ornament which was spread over some of the later buildings.

The domes of Bijapur are, as a rule, lost, internally, in their own gloom ; they have seldom any clerestory lights, and, where they do exist, as in the mosque at the Ibrahim

Rauza, they are too low. The domes of Ahmedabad are raised above the general roof upon pillars, and the light and air are freely admitted. In some of the high stilted domes here, the ceilings are carried up so far, inside of them, that it is almost impossible to see them for the gloom which ever fills them; they are more like great dark circular caverns hanging over head. In these cases, which are so frequent, the best corrective would have been double doming, the inner or lower dome forming the ceiling. But this device is met with nowhere, save in the Ibrahim Rauza, where a curious flat intervening ceiling, between the floor and dome, takes the place of an inner dome,* and which really produces a second storey. As a rule, the interior was sacrificed to the exterior without any attempt being made to correct the defect. Where the diameter of the domical ceiling is great compared with its height, as in the best examples, light enough is admitted to show the ceilings; but there are scores of examples where the interior height is from two to three times the diameter of the dome, so that little light can reach them, and they are thus great hollow cylinders.

It may be mentioned, in connection with the domes, that all those of the state buildings of Bijapur are, or have been, surmounted with brazen finials bearing the crescent, the Turkish emblem, declaring the origin of the Adil Shahi family.

---

* That double doming was known and practised by the Muhammadans, is evident from the occurrence of one at Bagdad, near the river. See plate p. 131, *The Euphrates and the Tigris*. T. Nelson & Sons, London.

The arches are, as a rule, two-centred. Sometimes they are struck from a single centre; and the curves are carried up from the springing to a point in the haunches, whence tangents are struck to the crown. This is the prevailing form of arch, but others are in use as well. We find the true *ogee* arch, the Gothic arch, the segmental, and, in one case at least, an almost flat arch. They are sometimes built with rough voussoirs, and sometimes corbelled forward from the adjoining masonry. They are often ornamented with richly moulded cusps, as in Ali Shahid Pir's mosque, and then look particularly well.

Another prominent feature are the graceful minarets, that flank the mosques and rise above the corners of some of the tombs. These are, with the exception of a pair, which are rather towers than minarets, attached to the Makka mosque, entirely ornamental; they are not like the Ahmedabad and Gujarat ones, receptacles for staircases leading to galleries round them, at different heights, from which to call to prayer. They are purely ornamental adjuncts to the façade, and are rather more attenuated than those of Gujarat.

Excepting in the case of the two converted Hindu temples in the citadel, and the guard-rooms at the gateway, there is no other example of the pillar and lintel style which was practised so much in Gujarat.

The Gol Gumbaz.—By far the largest and most conspicuous building in Bijapur is the mausoleum of Muhammad Adil Shah (or Mahmud as he is sometimes called.) In the time of the "Merry Monarch," Bijapur attained its zenith of architectural greatness. Luxury held her court within its walls and the Sultan and his nobles worshipped at her shrine. One of the first concerns of the king, on ascending the *masnad*, was the building of his own tomb ; and this he set about at once, so that he might complete it before he died. In this there was, naturally, great rivalry, for each monarch wished to leave such a tomb behind him as would eclipse those of his predecessors, leave no room for improvement to his successors, and so single out his name conspicuously from them all. And Muhammad certainly succeeded in doing this in a manner beyond anything attempted before or after him. Ibrahim II., his father, had just been buried in his own tomb, the like of which was not to be found anywhere in the Dekhan. With its lavish abundance of decoration, gilded and gorgeously coloured, its slender and graceful minarets, its exquisite proportions, and its surroundings of lovely gardens, it made his father's simple tomb sink into insignificance, and become a hovel beside it. Here was a puzzle for this "Old King Cole." How was he to surpass it? In this last work, the architects and builders had done their very best; they could do no more in that line. The only thing left to him, then, was to substitute quantity for quality. If he could not surpass the delicate chiselling and lacelike balustrades of the Ibrahim Rauza, he would, at least, build such a tomb as would, by its immense size, dwarf this and every other building in the city—a tomb that would arrest the eye from every quarter for miles around, and carry with it the name of Muhammad, the great Sultan Muhammad.

The general appearance of the building is that of a great cube, surmounted by a huge hemispherical dome, with an octogonal tower at each of its four corners, these being crowned by smaller domes. The only prominent feature on the faces of the building is the great deep overhanging cornice, which, at a high level, runs round all four sides. The doorways, small lancet windows, and surface decoration, by no means assert themselves, and, from a short distance off, are hardly noticed on the bare looking walls. The monotony of this, however, is broken by the towers, which are riddled with arched openings from base to summit—seven in each of the seven stories into which each tower is divided. The crest of the walls, above the cornice, is crenellated. The diameter of the dome is rather less than the breadth of the building. A winding staircase ascends in each of the corners of the building just where the towers abut on to it, and, communicating with each storey of the towers, at last leads out on to the flat roof, between the corners and the dome. Passages lead from the roof, through the thickness of the dome, into the whispering gallery around the interior of the same.

The dome is practically a hemisphere of 124 feet 5 inches interior diameter. The thickness of the same at the springing is 10 feet, whilst near the crown it is 9 feet. Thus the total external diameter at the springing is 144 feet. The curves of the surface are nowhere perfect, so that the measurements taken across different diameters vary several inches. The great compartment below, which is covered by the dome, is 135 feet 5 inches square at the floor level, and this gives an area of 18,337·67 square feet, from which if we take 228·32 square feet for the projecting angles of the piers carrying the cross arches, which stand out from the walls into the floor, two on each face, we get a total covered area, uninterrupted by supports of any kind, of 18,109·35 square feet. This is the largest space covered by a single dome in the world, the next largest being that of the Pantheon at Rome, of 15.833 square feet.

The total exterior height of the building, above the platform on which it stands, is 198 feet 6 inches exclusive of the wooden pole at the top. But this, when it held the gilt finial, formed part of the building, and another 8 feet must be allowed for it; this would give an extreme height of 206 feet 6 inches. The interior height from the level of the floor, around the tomb platform, to the top of the dome, is 178 feet. The drop from the gallery to the floor below is 109 feet 6 inches.

In this colossal mausoleum we have the system of the *pendentives*, used with such effect throughout the Bijapur buildings, displayed to its greatest advantage. Theoretically there is no limit to the size of the building that could be raised and covered in on these principles. But, with the material the Bijapur builders had, it is very doubtful whether they could have erected a larger building without great risk of accidents. Here they had no trouble with their foundations for they had selected a spot where the solid rock comes to the surface, and the whole of the foundations are planted upon it. One of the greatest troubles and risks, that of subsequent unequal settling, that the builders of great and heavy works have often to contend with, did not exist here.

"In a spherical roof intersected with groined compartments, the term *pendentives* was applied to the surfaces included between such compartments. The same term is applied to the surfaces included in the angles formed by a groined vaulting at its spring." It is in the latter sense that it is used in the Bijapur buildings. The *pendentives* are thus a result of cross arching or groining. The accompanying diagram explains the arrangement. ABCD is the square room to be covered in. Points are taken in the walls at E, F, G, H, K, L, M, and N so that they form the corners of an octagon. At these points buttresses of piers are built up the walls to carry arches. The latter are then thrown across, from one pier to an alternate pier, so that the arches, thus constructed, form, in plan, two intersecting squares EGKM and FHLN, and the crowns of all the arches fall upon a circle inscribed within these

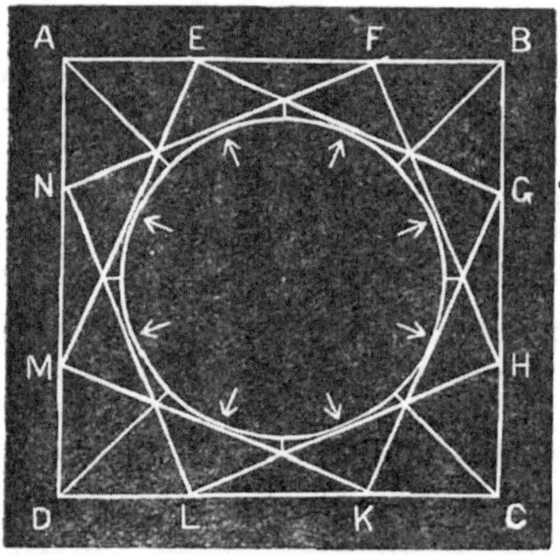

squares, and carry the dome which may be as small, in internal diameter, as this circle. It will thus be seen that the dome rests directly upon the crowns of the arches, which are always pointed; and the former, being a solid mass of concrete, like a shell, with no loose voussoirs, rests as a dead weight upon the crowns of the arches, conveying no outward thrust to them. The lines joining the intersections and points of the arches, and the corners of the outer square, cut up the space, between the circle and these corners, into a number of concave spherical triangles. These are the *pendentives*.

On the great raised platform in the centre of the building, under the dome, are the counterfeit tombs of the grandson of Sultan Muhammad, his younger wife Arus Bibi, the Sultan himself, his favourite mistress Rhumba, his daughter, and his older wife, in this order from east to west. The real tombs, where the bodies lie, are in the vaults immediately below these, the entrance to which is by a staircase under the western entrance. Over Muhammad's tomb is erected a wooden canopy.

A most remarkable feature of this building is its whispering gallery. This, as mentioned before, runs round the interior of the dome on a level with its springing, and hangs out from the walls into the building. It is about 11 feet wide, the dome itself forming the back wall of the same. On entering the building one is struck with the loud echoes that fill the place in answer to his footfall; but these sounds are much intensified on entering the gallery. The footfall of a single person is enough to awaken the echoes of the tread of a regiment; strange weird sounds, and mocking whispers, emanate from the wall around. Loud laughter is answered by a score of fiends, for, upon our entrance, the elfin band retreated precipitately behind the plaster of the wall. The slightest whisper is heard from side to side; and a conversation can be easily carried on across the diameter of the dome, in the lowest undertone. A single loud clap is echoed over ten times, distinctly.

Instances of multiple echoes, such as this, are the Pantheon, the tomb of Metella, the wife of Crassus, which is said to have repeated a whole verse of the Æneid as many as eight times, and the whispering gallery of St. Paul's. It is not at all likely, as some suppose, that the architect of this building had the production of a good echo in view when he constructed the dome, for it is no more than a duplicate of many a dome in Bijapur, on a much larger scale, with nothing extra about it in any way. The echo was, no doubt, a purely natural result of the size of the dome. In the smaller domes we get what is called resonance, their diameters not being sufficiently great to allow of a distinct echo. It requires rather more than 65 feet, between a person and the reflecting surface, so that the sound, on return, may reach his ear immediately upon the dying out of the original sound, and so create the impression of a second sound—an echo. If a greater distance intervenes, the echo is more distinct, as more time separates the original sound from the reflected sound. If the distance is less, no distinct echo results, as the original and reflected sounds overlap and produce a confused sound or resonance.

From the roof of the tomb, surrounding the dome, a most extensive view of the whole city is obtained. To the south-west is the Jami Masjid, conspicuous among its surrounding buildings; more to the west may be seen Mustafa Khan's mosque, the Asar Mahal, with its great open front, and the many buildings in the citadel, most prominent, among which, is the Anand Mahal. Directly west is, first, the unfinished mausoleum of Ali (II.) Adil Shah, with its rows of skeleton arches, then the lofty Haidar Burj, with the old Dekhani Idgah beside it. Away, beyond the walls, are the domes and *minars* of the Ibrahim Rauza, and the white dome of the Amin Dargah with the Sarai (Jail) and scores of surrounding buildings. Out to the east is the unfinished tomb of Jahan Begam and the tomb of Ain-ul-Mulk.

Over the south doorway, below, and inside, there is a large boldly cut inscription in three compartments. Each of these three sections is a complete sentence in itself, and each, on computing the values of the Persian letters, gives the date A.H. 1067 (A.D. 1656), the date of Muhammad's death. These sentences are:—

"The end of Muhammad has become laudable."
"Muhammad Sultan whose abode is in paradise."
"The abode of peace became Muhammad Shah."

The portion added to the back, or north side, of the building, is said to have been intended to afford a resting place for Jahan

Begam, the Queen of Muhammad Shah, but, whatever it was built for, it was never finished and never occupied. An inspection of the masonry shows that it was added after the main building was erected. In building the walls of the Gol Gumbaz, the builders appear to have first erected four great arches, and then to have walled up their open spaces, so that an addition, such as the above, could have been easily added at any subsequent time, and the filling in, under one of the great arches, knocked out, to give access to it, without impairing the building. Below it, is a vault, corresponding, in plan, to the upper chamber, which goes far to show that it was intended for a tomb.

Standing out before the Gol Gumbaz, on its south side, is the great gateway, over which was the *Nagarkhana*, where the music was played at stated times. It appears never to have been finished, as its *minars* were not carried up beyond the roof. This has now been converted into a Museum, to house objects found in Bijapur and the country round.

On the west, and standing on the edge of the platform, is the well proportioned mosque attached to the tomb, which was, for many years, used as a travellers' bungalow, until Lord Curzon rescued it from this degrading use and caused it to be vacated and restored. It is an elegant building with a rich, deep cornice, but much damaged, and slender well-proportioned minarets. The stairways leading to the roof, as in most of the Bijapur mosques, are in the thickness of the end walls. In this they differ very much from the Ahmedabad buildings, where the stair is, almost invariably, a spiral passage winding up through the minarets. Two adjuncts were necessary to every Muhammadan tomb, namely, a mosque and a tank. Here we find two tanks, one before the main entrance to the tomb, and another between the latter and the mosque. The general style, finish, and proportions of this mosque shew clearly that it was not due to the want of cunning artisans that the Gol Gumbaz was built so plainly, and was covered with plaster, instead of being decorated with a profusion of chiselled stone-work. Moreover, there are parts about the great tomb itself, the great cornice, and the cornices of the little *minars* on the top, which indicate the presence of skilled workmen in stone. Its severity of outline and decoration was thus designedly so, and was the outcome of an ambition to overshadow all previous work by simple mass, which has resulted, almost, in clumsiness.

The Jami Masjid.—This building, the principal mosque in the city, is situated in the middle of the south-east quarter of the town. It stands upon the south side of the road leading from the Allahpur gate to the citadel. Including the great open courtyard, embraced between its two wings, it occupies the greatest area of any building in Bijapur—about 91,000 square feet to the bases of the towers at the ends of the wings, beyond which there is a further extension up to the eastern gateway, bringing up the total covered area to 116,300 square feet. The main building, the mosque proper, is built across the west end of the great court. The massive square piers, which support the roof, divide the length of the façade into nine bays, and the depth into five, which would give a total of forty-five bays in the body of the mosque; but nine in the centre are taken up by the open space under the great dome, *i.e.*, the four central piers being absent, a great square area is enclosed by the surrounding twelve piers. Over this space, and towering above the flat roof, rises the dome. A full description of the manner in which this, and the majority of the Bijapur domes, are supported has already been given in the account of the Gol Gumbaz.

The dome of the Jami Masjid is generally looked upon as the best proportioned in Bijapur. It is a true dome, and is not, what many are in the town, a sham; it is the roof of a domical ceiling. Perhaps we test it too much by European models when passing such favourable judgement upon it. The bulbous dome, so characteristic of Saracenic architecture, is foreign to Christendom. Our domes are, as a rule, segmental, or are intended to appear so when constructed. Now the Jami Masjid dome is segmental, hence it pleases the European eye more than the bulbous ones do. But this is hardly a fair way of judging it. As an example of Saracenic architecture, it must be judged by what is best in that order; and, using this test, it will probably be found to err as much in being too flat, as many others do by being too elongated and strangled at the neck. It would have been improved had it been raised four or five feet out of the square upon which it rests. One of the most perfect in outline, as a Saracenic dome, is that over the tomb of Ain-ul-Mulk, to the east of the town; and, next to this, is that of Khawas Khan's tomb, one of the "Two Sisters."

The interior of the mosque, save the decorated *mehrab*, is severely plain. There is a quiet simplicity about it which adds much to the impressive solemnity of the place. The walls and piers are all faced with white plaster. High up in the back walls, and the walls of the wings, is a row of small windows, filled with geometric tracery in perforated stone. Before the *mehrab* hangs a great thick curtain, and, when this is drawn aside, a sight of gorgeous splendour is revealed. The whole front and recess of the *mehrab* is covered with rich gilding upon a coloured ground. There are representations of tombs and minarets, censers and chains, niches with books in them, vases with flowers, and the whole is interspersed with bands and medallions bearing inscriptions. These are as follows:—

> "Place no trust in life: it is but brief,"
> "There is no rest in this transitory world."
> "The world is very pleasing to the senses."
> "Life is the best of all gifts, but it is not lasting,"
> "Malik Yaqub, a servant of the mosque, and the slave of Sultan Muhammad completed the mosque."
> "This gilding and ornamental work was done by order of the Sultan Muhammad Adil Shah, A.H. 1045." (A.D. 1636)

As the mosque was commenced by Ali (I) Adil Shah it will thus be seen, that the decoration of the *mehrab* was no portion of the original design. The colouring of this part was conceived, and carried out, by Sultan Muhammad, who appears to have been very partial to painted decoration. He adorned the walls of the Asar Mahal, and the painting in the water pavilion at Kumatgi is probably his work. He also gilded and decorated the walls of the Sat Manjli, the abode of his favourite mistress, Rhumba. Surface decoration, in colour, was used in the tombs of Ali I. and Ibrahim II.; but it was confined to geometric patterns and conventional foliage. It was not until the time of Muhammad, when the prohibition against it was disregarded, that figure painting was introduced into Muhammadan buildings.

The floor of the mosque has been most carefully plastered and polished, and divided, by thin black lines, into compartments, each of which is supposed to accommodate one worshipper. Altogether there are over 2,250 such spaces. These are in the body of the mosque, and the wings are not taken into account. The wings were probably never intended for worshippers. It is said that these divisions were ordered by the Emperor Aurangzib, who is also said to have built the large gateway on the east side of the courtyard.

High up, round the outside of the building, runs a deep corridor, and it is mainly the arches of this corridor that break the monotony of the sombre plain walls of the exterior.

The Mehtar Mahal.—On the south side of the road, between the Jami Masjid and the Citadel gate, and nearer the latter, stands one of the prettiest little buildings in Bijapur, Though called a Mahal, or palace, it is really a gateway to the inner courtyard of a mosque, with upper rooms and balconies, where men might assemble and converse, and, from its windows, enjoy the different views of the city. The principal object of the group, the mosque within, is a neat little building, and it would have attracted far more attention than it now does had it not been so close to the more ambitious design—the gateway. The general outline of the latter is that of a tall, square, tower, surmounted by two slender minarets at its upper forward corners. The main entrance runs through the centre of the ground floor, another floor, and an open terrace, being above it, with balconied windows projecting from the surfaces of the building. The most ornate feature about the gateway are these windows. They are bay or oriel windows, the projecting landing, or sill, being supported, beneath, by bracketing ornamented with rows of hanging buds or drops, the brackets, or consoles, being themselves connected into a whole by decorated transverse tie-pieces in ascending tiers. The balcony parapet, with its rosette panels and neat capping, is carried across the face of the building, and serves its purpose to two little side windows. From this rise three lancet-shaped lights in the front, and one each in the ends; and, from the mullions between these, project a row of most richly wrought stone brackets supporting the deep overhanging cornice. They are exceedingly thin, long, rectangular, slabs, perforated and worked over with the most beautiful arabesque. They are such as one would expect to find in woodwork, and look far too delicate to be wrought in brittle stone; but they have lasted, without breaking, for nearly three hundred years, during the most part of which time the building has not been cared for. The hanging fringe on the cornice above, has, unfortunately, been mostly knocked away, but a few little bits remain to shew how pretty it was. The face of the building, from the window upwards, is ornamented with lancet-shaped panels, corresponding in size to the lights of the window, but below this, and around the doorway, the whole surface is embellished with some exceedingly neat surface ornament. Up the two flanks of the face of the building, rise the octagonal buttresses of the minarets, with horizontal mouldings and cornices at the levels of the different floors. Along the crest of the building, between the minarets, was a most beautifully perforated parapet, but this, too, had suffered very much. Its slabs were easily removed, and were probably carried off, in days gone by, when the relics of Bijapur were a prey to the occasional visitor, and a quarry to the local builders, whose very familiarity with these unused buildings blunted their respect for them; at a time when this old deserted city was lying almost in oblivion, uncared for and desolate. This parapet has lately been renewed.

Passing within, we enter a compartment, through the centre of which, between the two raised platforms, is the passage to the courtyard. The most noteworthy thing here is the very curiously arranged ceiling. This, as well as the ceiling of the upper floor, is constructed in the same manner as that at the Ibrahim Rauza, which is fully described in the account of that building. The old wooden doorway is worth inspection, with its heavy massive framing and quaint iron bosses and nails. Some similar iron work, very prettily perforated, may be seen on the door of the tomb of Shah Karim, near the south-east corner of the Jami Masjid. The Mehtar Mahal is about 24 feet square in plan, and 66 feet to the tops of the minarets.

The mosque is a neat little building; it had a very fine cornice and brackets, and has a rich parapet along the top. The minarets, however, are not quite in keeping with the rest. They are very primitive looking and inelegant, and compare very unfavourably with those of the gateway. From the roof upwards, they are exceedingly plain, being nothing more than tall tapering round shafts, with a row of leaves, about half way up, to relieve their monotony of outline. They are not even surmounted by the usual large ball or bulbous finial, but are plainly rounded off with a very small ball and trident. This latter is an unusual device. There are so many points of resemblance between this mosque and that of Malika Jahan Begam (or the Janjiri mosque as it is also called) that one cannot help thinking there was some connection between the builders of that mosque and this. The Janjiri mosque is generally ascribed to Ibrahim II., and is said to have been erected in 1587.

There are several very unreliable stories current accounting for the origin of the name of the Mehtar Mahal. It is just possible this is not the original name at all, but one subsequently applied to it, meaning the "Superior" Mahal, and given to it to indicate its surpassing beauty; it is more likely that the mosque and gateway were originally called after him, who caused them to be erected. Then, as it was probably private property, and the great door was usually closed against intruders, the mosque became lost sight of, and the gateway, whose upper rooms were often used, was raised to the dignity of a Mahal. One story ascribes its origin to a sweeper, who was unexpectedly enriched by the king in fulfilment of a vow, and who, not knowing what to do with so much money, built this Mahal, which was on this account called the Mehtar or Sweeper's Mahal. It would hardly have accorded with Muhammadan ideas of decency, to have allowed a sweeper to erect a mosque; and there is no doubt at all that the mosque and gate were built by the same person. We may dismiss this story as absurd. Another credits one Mehtar Gada, a fakir, in the time of Ibrahim II., with the building of it, but the details of this story are also very improbable.

That the mosque and gateway were built at the same time is evident from the fact that a peculiar kind of stone, found nowhere else in Bijapur, so far as I am aware, is used in the back wall of the mosque and the upper chamber of the gateway. On the Andu Masjid, described further on, and which is of much the same style of work, though less profusely decorated, we have the date of its erection given as 1608.

On the little pavilion before the Arash Mahal, which is covered with precisely the same kind of surface decoration as is used on the face of the Mehtar Mahal, we have the date, twice over, 1669. The masonry is of the same class as that of the Andu Masjid and the Mehtar Mahal. I would be inclined to place the latter between these two, and do not think 1620 far wrong as the probable date of its erection.

The Asar Mahal.—Upon the outer edge of the citadel moat, towards the east, and facing in that direction, is one of the most inelegant buildings, yet the most sacred, in Bijapur—the Asar Mahal or Palace of the Relic. In one of the rooms, within, are supposed to be enshrined two hairs of the Prophet's beard. Many years ago, burglars broke into this room one night and rather disarrranged its contents; and, as the opening of the relic box is forbidden, and the room itself is only opened once a year, no one can be sure that the thieves were pious enough to leave the gold mounted relic tube in the box. The Muhammadans, now, would rather not meddle with it, but prefer to believe it there, than risk the opening and find their fondest hopes dispelled. Interested parties derive a certain amount of benefit from visitors and pilgrims to the shrine, and would not be likely, even if they knew, to do or say anything to undo the sanctity of the place.

The general shape of the building is that of a great rectangular box laid over on its side, its lid removed, and the open front turned toward the east. The depth of the building, from front to back, is divided into a forward hall, occupying the whole length and height of the building, and a set of two-storeyed rooms filling the whole length of the back half. These rooms are two deep, and the best apartment in the place is the long central one upstairs, towards the back, which is 81 feet long by 27 feet broad. A doorway leads out, through the east side of this, into a gallery, with open front, looking into the great hall below. In the room off the north side of this gallery, the relic is supposed to be enshrined. The two rooms, to the south, are the principal show rooms of the place. The three doors leading out of the gallery, which is known as the Gilded Hall, on account of its ceiling having been covered with gold leaf, are worth notice. They are, perhaps, the best works of art, next the carpets, in the building. Like all native doors, they consist of two leaves, with chain and ring above for fastening them. But the whole surface of each has been ribbed out with blackwood into geometric patterns and borders, and the little panels so formed are of ivory. They have, unfortunately, been subjected to rough use, and mischievous fingers have assisted to make them the wrecks they are. Most of the ivory panels have disappeared.

Entering the room to the south, we find ourselves in a gorgeously painted apartment. The walls are covered with the interminable windings of the stems, leaves, and flowers of a blue creeper. On the backs of the niches, are painted vases and urns containing flowers, and the ceiling, and its beams, have also been profusely decorated. A good deal of gilding remains on the walls, and, like that on the ceiling of the hall outside this room, retains its lustre remarkably well. This is sufficient proof of the purity of the gold leaf used, otherwise it would have tarnished long ere this. The next room, beyond this, is also elaborately painted, but in a different style, the lower portions of the walls being covered with figures, which have been so damaged, that it is difficult to make out the separate forms, and impossible to solve the stories of the scenes portrayed. From what can be seen, they savour very strongly of western handicraft, and, indeed, in one instance, regular European wine glasses are represented. These paintings were probably done by European artists in the employ of Sultan Muhammad, who, on their arrival, had little knowledge of eastern manners, customs, or traditions, and had, therefore, to fall back upon western ideas and mythology for subjects, and then clothe them, as far as they were able, in Indian habiliments. Paintings of figures, like images, are never tolerated by strict Muhammadans; and, it is said, that Aurangzib was so incensed at seeing these upon the walls of a Muhammadan building, claiming a certain degree of sanctity, that he ordered the faces of all the figures to be destroyed. The upper parts of the walls are painted to represent trees, sky, and clouds. In this room are two large boxes, containing a great number of coverings for the relic box, curtains, and other hangings in silk and kinkob, which have been carelessly kept, are falling into rags, and are sadly moth-eaten. The fine old Persian carpets, which are also badly used, especially at the *Urus* ceremony, when they are trodden upon by hundreds of dirty feet, are generally kept in the large room behind the Gilded Hall. Beside these, there are other articles of olden times, such as old china candlesticks, quaint copper kettles and pans, and some old glass bottles, but nothing among them of any merit as works of art.

The geometric tracery of the upper parts of the windows, up-stairs, is very neat. In the last two rooms, some of the yellow and blue stained glass still remains in them, but, from all the rest, it has gone or was never inserted. The rail along the front of the Gilded Hall is neat and very appropriate. Notice the ingenious device of perforated wavy lines, radiating from a centre, in the tops of some of the back windows, to represent, with a strong light shining through them, the rays of the setting sun.

Returning down-stairs, we pass the closed door of a room on the left, near the foot of the staircase. This was the *kitabkhana*, or library, and the room is lined all round with small cupboards in which the old Asar Mahal MSS were once kept, the bulk of which are said to have been carted away by Aurungzib. The other rooms, on tke ground floor, are all dirty lumber rooms. In the one below the relic chamber, and before which is the curtain and wooden platform, is a model of the tomb of Muhammad at Medina. It is a curious looking thing but a very poor piece of work, very similar, in appearance, to a nursery Noah's Ark. It is carefully stowed away in a huge chest.

The general aspect of the great hall, if ever worth much, has been ruined by two tall Gothic arches, built across it, very many years ago, to strengthen the roof. The outer edge of the roof is supported by four huge teak pillars. The ceiling is neatly panelled in wood, in geometric patterns, and has been painted in light tints.

Before the building is a great square tank, always kept full, it being fed by the Begam Talao and Torweh conduits; and, it is the addition of this, with its reflections and ripple, that, in a measure, makes up for the bare looking exterior of the palace itself.

Built by Muhammad Shah about 1646, it was originally intended as a hall of justice, butShah Jahan, it is said, obliged him to abandon the idea of having his court of justice, the Dad Mahal, as it was first called, outside the citadel walls. The building was, subsequently, made the resting place of the relic of the Prophet, which had, before this, been brought to Bijapur by Mir Muhammad Salli Hamadani from Makka. To make the place more accessible for its original purpose, a viaduct was constructed across the moat, supported upon substantial piers, connecting the interior of the citadel with the back of the buiding; and entrance to the latter was gained through door-ways, off different levels of the viaduct, into both the lower and upper floors. Right in the middle of the roadway, on the viaduct, and above the citadel walls, is a water cistern, where it was probably intended to wash the feet before entering the hall.

Beside the Asar Mahal, on the north, are the remains of a contiguous building called the Jahaz Mahal, from it is said, its fancied resemblance to a ship, but it certainly has nothing about it now which would remind one of a ship.* It is also said that, in this building, were the offices of the admiralty, hence Jahaz Mahal or admiralty office; and we know Bijapur possessed a considerable fleet at one time. With bare walls and hollow gaping doors and windows, from which all its old woodwork has gone, it is a wreck. It is in two storeys, the lower ground floor being divided, by a central wall, into an outer and inner arcade, with a transverse room on either side of the central gateway. At the ends of the building, on the outer sides, are cook rooms, while, on the inner sides, are staircases leading up to the upper storey. The upper floor was divided into suites of rooms, the walls of which are filled with pigeon-hole niches. Below, in the middle of the building, is the great gateway leading into the Asar Mahal, the ponderous wooden gates of which still swing in their sockets, and the huge cylindrical wooden beam, which held the door fast behind, still lies upon its numerous rollers in its long socket in the wall behind the door. On the east side of the enclosure of the Asar Mahal are the ruins of a smaller building called the Pani Mahal, or "Water Palace."

* There is a Jahaz Mahal at Mandu, in Central India, situated between two large tanks, the two sheets of water, in imagination, forming one on which the palace floats like a ship or *jahaz*.

The Taj Bauri.—This, the largest tank in Bijapur, is situated in the west of the town, near the Makka gate. The entrance to the tank, facing the north, is spanned by a high arch 35 feet across. Upon either side of this, and standing forward, is a two-storeyed octagonal tower surmounted by a dome. East and west of these run long arcades which were intended for the accommodation of travellers. Descending the broad flight of steps, between the towers, and passing under the great arch, we come upon a landing which juts out into the water of the tank, from which flights of steps, on either side, lead down to the water's edge. The tank itself is 223 feet square. Around the inner side of the high wall that encloses it, runs a narrow gallery or terrace with a low parapet wall on the inner side. This communicates with sets of rooms, in the middle of each of the three sides, which overlook the tank, those on the south side being converted into a Hindu shrine dedicated to Baladev. Here, in one corner, are congregated scores of brass gods of all sizes, shapes, and names. Vishnu and his belongings are mixed up pretty freely with Siva and his, and a well-nigh naked *bairagi* attends to them. Above the sides of the tank are arrangements for raising water, those on the south being still used to irrigate the gardens behind.

There are different stories told about the construction of this work. One says it was built by Malik Sandal, the architect of the Ibrahim Rauza, in honour of Taj Sultana, the Queen of Ibrahim II., in the year 1620. Another affirms that Sultan Muhammad, having done Malik Sandal a great injustice, and wishing to make reparation for the same, asked him to name anything he liked and he would grant it him. Having no children, through whom to transmit his name to posterity, he asked that he might be allowed to construct some substantial piece of work by which his name might be perpetuated. This was granted, and the king himself supplied him with the necessary funds. Had this been the case, he would hardly have left the tank without an inscription setting forth his own praises ; and, if constructed for the purpose mentioned, it would, no doubt, have borne his name. The first account is more likely the true one, and, as Chand Bibi had already a tank constructed in her name in the city, it is very likely, indeed, that Taj Sultana, the Queen of the reigning king, wished to have one too, but a finer one if possible.

The Malik-i-Maidan.—Upon the largest bastion of the western ramparts of the city, situated about midway between the Makka and Shahapur gates, lies the famous Malik-i-Maidan or "Monarch of the Plain," which, next to the great iron gun, the Landa Kasab, is the largest in Bijapur. It differs from this last, and most of the other guns, in that it is a casting in gun or bell metal or some similar alloy. It is more like a huge howitzer than anything else, being a great thick dumpy piece with a calibre very large in proportion to its length, and which spreads slightly from the breech to the muzzle, allowing a very great amount of windage. It is thus evident that it could not have been used with anything like precision of aim, even at close quarters, leaving its carrying capacity out of the question. Like "Mons Meg" at Edinburgh, it has a smaller chamber for the powder, and this was no doubt intended to give the gun greater thickness where the greatest strength was required. The surface of the gun has been chased after casting, the necessary excrescences of metal for this purpose being allowed for. The muzzle of the gun has been worked into the shape of the head of a dragon with open jaws, between the sharp curved teeth of which are small elephants, one on either side of the muzzle. The tip of the nose forms the foresight, and the small ears are drilled and thus converted into rings to attach tackle to. There are three inscriptions on the top; one records the name of the man who made it, viz., Muhammad *bin* Hassan, Rumi, another gives the date of its casting as A.H. 956 (A.D. 1549) with the name of Abdul Ghazi Nizam Shah, and the third, a later inscription, was added by Aurangzib when he conquered Bijapur in A.H. 1097 (A.D. 1685-86) recording that event.

The measurements of the gun have been often taken, and almost as often have they varied. This is accounted for by its slight irregularity in shape, one side being longer than the other, and its calibre a little more or less one way than another. It measures 14 feet 4 inches long, with a maximum diameter of 4 feet 11 inches. Its bore at the muzzle is 2 feet 4 inches, and 2 feet 2 inches at shoulder of powder chamber.

It will be seen from the above measurements that, in firing ball, there would be at least one inch windage at the muzzle round the ball, owing to the spread of the bore, and it is very evident that no approach to accurate practice could have been made even at short ranges. But, in spite of this, the gun has been credited with the most wonderful performances. The best story of all is perhaps the following. It is said that, during Aurangzib's siege of the town, he was observed from the walls by Sikandar seated by the cistern in the Ibrahim Rauza, washing his feet before going into the mosque to pray. Sikandar, wishing to take advantage of his opportunity, ordered his gunner, Gulamdas, to charge the Malik-i-Maidan with ball and fire upon him. The gunner was, however, unwilling to take the life of the Emperor, but, to make Sikandar think he did actually try, he aimed as near as he could to Aurangzib, with the result that he knocked the *lota* he was using out of his hand. Considering the distance, which is fully half a mile, and the short spreading bore of the gun, this story is worth recording for the very impudent assurance with which it is told. It is much more likely the gun was used to fire grapeshot down upon soldiery at close quarters, and the fine scoring of the bore confirms this view. It is said they generally rammed in bags of thick double pice (copper coins) and fired them, and this is not at all improbable.

The Malik-i-Maidan was cast at Ahmednagar, and the place where this operation was carried out is still shewn. It is said to have done considerable execution at the battle of Talikot, having been taken there with Nizam Shah's artillery.

Subsequently, it was mounted on the hill fort of Parandah, one of Nizam Shah's strongholds, fifty miles to the north west of Sholapur, and one hundred miles north of Bijapur. But when this place fell into the hands of Bijapur in 1632 the gun was brought away as a trophy of war. But this grand old gun was nearly meeting a sad fate as lately as 1854. About that year the Satara Commissioner ordered the sale of useless dead stock lying about Bijapur, and the Mamlatdar, acting up to the letter of these instructions, put the Monarch up to auction ! The highest bid for this mass of metal was one hundred and fifty rupees, and the Mamlatdar, considering this very little for so much material, reported the bid to the Assistant Commissioner, and pointed out that the gun was held in great veneration by people far and wide. Upon this, the Assistant Commissioner cancelled the sale, and directed that the gun should be retained. Later, a proposal was made to transport the gun to the British Museum, but the Fates wisely ordered otherwise, and it still remains upon the walls it protected in days gone by.

The gun was mounted upon a wrought-iron Y-support, which turned on a pivot let into the centre of a stone platform, part of which support still remains, together with a travelling transverse trollie or carriage of some kind, whose wheels ran in channels in the platform. These channels are segments of circles, diametrically opposite each other, starting forward, on each side, from the recoil wall. This wall, which is a circular piece of solid masonry at the back of the gun, was built to counteract its recoil, and thus prevent damage to the pivot or carriage. The end of the gun very nearly touches the wall, enough room being left for free movement; at the time of firing this space was wedged up tightly.

The large Sherza Burj, so named from the lions which are carved upon it, just above the one on which the gun rests, was evidently built as a higher and better platform for this gun; but the latter was never placed upon it. The radius of the circle, from centre to recoil wall, is the same as on the lower turret; and the large hole for the pivot, one foot and half an inch in diameter, corresponds with that below. The masonry is carefully dressed and well laid while that of the lower platform is very poor, and has the appearance of having been hurriedly built in order to get the gun planted with as little delay as possible. The higher and stronger turret was more deliberately planned and built. Upon it is an inscription which tells us that the turret* was built in A.H. 1069 (A.D. 1658) during the reign of Ali (II.) Adil Shah, by the king himself, and was made firm as a rock in five months. In the upper platform is a small well which was intended to hold water for washing out the gun, and, behind the turret, are the remains of small tanks and a magazine.

---

*Not the bastion as is generally translated. The bastion, on which this turret stands, holds three gun platforms—the old and new ones for the Malik-i-Maidan, and a smaller one for a small gun.

This gun, like all the others, has been dismounted, and its carriage has been carried away. From the manner in which these dismounted guns have been carefully placed on huge timbers, it would appear to have been deliberately done by an enemy, after capturing the city, perhaps by Aurangzib when he finally conquered Bijapur, who, when he left, carried away the carriages with the intention of bringing them back for his own use, should he have occasion, again, to return to Bijapur. In the meantime the guns would be next to useless without them. Had occasion required, it would have been an easier matter to have slipped the carriages in under the guns, supported as they were on these blocks, than it would have been had they been carelessly thrown down or perhaps tumbled into the ditch. Aurangzib did remain in the city for some years after its capture, and, on his departure, may have thought of returning, as it is said he entertained the idea of making Bijapur his capital for this part of India, in which case, he would again have needed the guns upon their carriages.

It is said that two guns were cast in the same mould, and that the other one was sunk in the Bhima or Krishna, on its way to the battle of Talikot, if it is true they were ever taken there. It was named the Kadak Bijjali, which, in vulgar parlance, might be translated "greased lightning."

The Haidar Burj.—This is a solitary tower, standing upon high ground in the west of the town, and not far from the Malik-i-Maidan. It is the highest gun platform in Bijapur, and is a very conspicuous object for miles around. It is also called the Upri or Upli Burj. In plan it is an oval, its major axis running north and south. Round the south and east sides winds a stair, from the ground on the south-west to the top on the east of the tower. Let into the wall on the left, near the top, on the stairway, is a tablet, bearing a Persian inscription, which records the building of the tower by Haidar Khan, a general during the reigns of Ali Adil Shah and Ibrahim II.—no doubt the same man who built the Haidariah Mosque in 1583 near the Bari Kaman. This tower was also built in 1583, the sentence, giving the date, saying "This bastion is in the name of Haidar." The story of its construction says that Haidar Khan was absent from Bijapur, on the king's business, when Ali Adil Shah commanded each of his generals to assist in building the city walls. Haidar Khan, much to his disappointment, was thus precluded from taking any part in the erection of the city's defences. The king, Ibrahim, to please him in this matter, on his return, told him to construct a tower which should overtop the rest. It is easily seen that the story has resulted from the existence of the tower, and not the tower for the reasons set forth in the story. They made, or had got possession of, two extraordinarily long guns, and were puzzled to know what to do with them. It was clear, from their great length and comparatively small bore, that they were intended to carry a great distance. Placing them upon the low bastions of the walls would have crippled their capabilities, and would have made them of no more use than the shorter ones stationed there. The want of elevation in the wall bastions, and the undulating nature of the ground beyond them, prevented a good long range being obtained. It was then determined to build a specially high tower, and the high ground, on the north west of the town, close to the walls, presented itself as the best site. Haidar Khan undertook to build it, hence it bears his name.

These two guns still lie on the top of the tower. Two gun platforms, with recoil walls, were constructed for them, and, like all other guns, they were carried on carriages which revolved about a central pivot. The larger one is the longest piece of ordnance in Bijapur. It is 30 feet 8 inches long, and has a bore one foot in diameter. It was constructed of wrought iron bars, of square section, laid longitudinally about the bore, over which rings were slipped on, one at a time, and each welded with the last while red hot; as they cooled they shrank and bound the iron bars firmly together. In the whole length of the gun, there are over one hundred and fifty rings. Near the breech a second layer of rings has been put on to strengthen it, and, at the muzzle, a few extra projecting rings have been added to improve its appearance and give it a lip. This gun is called the Lamcharri or "Farflier." The other gun, which is constructed exactly like it, is 19 feet 10 inches long, with a bore of eight inches. It is possible these were brought on to the tower by means of an inclined plane, which was afterwards removed. A simpler method would have been to have laid the guns in position on the site, and to have carried them up with the tower as the latter was raised, course by course, and it is not unlikely this was the method adopted.

The tower shows signs of having been fired at from the west. Being close to the Malik-i-Maidan, which is on the walls beneath, it may have been struck by shot intended for the latter. From the top a good view of the city, and especially of the Shahapur suburb, is obtained.

Tomb of Ali (II.) Adil Shah.—The unfinished tomb of Ali (II.) Adil Shah lies a short distance to the north of the citadel and the Gagan Mahal. The great high basement, upon which the building stands, is 215 feet square. The basement of the Gol Gumbaz, or tomb of Muhammad Shah, is 158 feet square. The former, with the projecting corner buttresses, has a total width of face of 225 feet, while the latter, with its corner towers, measures 205 feet over all. This would, if completed, have been the greatest covered space in Bijapur. But, of course, the whole of this was not intended to be covered by a single dome; the central space only, 79 feet square, would have carried the main dome. This, judging from the plan of the piers attached to the walls, would have been worked inward from the square by cross-springers, and included pendentives, to an octagon, from which the dome would have risen. The diameter of the latter would not have exceeded 55 feet. Around the central area is a double arcade. The front façade of the Jami Masjid would represent, very nearly, each of the four façades of this tomb, with the dome rising from the centre. There would, no doubt, have been a number of small ornamental *minars* along the top, as in the tomb and mosque at the Ibrahim Rauza. The most peculiar characteristic of the building is its arches. They are purely Gothic in outline, being struck from two centres, with the curves continued up to the crown. The main characteristic of Bijapur arches is, that the curves, from the haunches, are only continued up to a certain point, from which the arch is a straight line to the crown, or, in many cases, a slightly inverted curve. The whole surface of the masonry has been left rough for a subsequent coating of plaster. On a raised platform, in the inner enclosure, is the tomb of Ali Adil Shah, while, in the south-west corner, on a little platform, is the tomb of a female, with the *bismillah* formulla written round it, which is said to be the tomb of Khurshe Khanam, the wife of Ali Adil Shah and mother of Sikander. Beside these two graves there are thirteen others, eleven of them being the graves of females. The very high basement would have added considerable dignity to the general effect of the finished building.

The Ibrahim Rauza.—The group of buildings, collectively known as the "Ibrahim Rauza," is situated a short distance to the west of the city, beyond the Makka gate. Upon a high platform, within a great square enclosure, are two large buildings facing one another, with a reservoir and fountain between them; and, between this platform and the surrounding walls, on three sides, is a level green sward, which at one time was a royal garden. The building on the east side of the platform is the tomb of Ibrahim (II.) Adil Shah, his queen Taj Sultana, and four other members of his family. In order, from east to west, the graves are those of Taj Sultana, wife of Ibrahim Padshah, Haji Badi Sahiba, his mother, Ibrahim Jagat-Gir, himself, Zohrah Sultana, his daughter, Darvesh Padshah, his son, and Sultan Salaman, another son.* The sepulchral chamber, which is 39 feet 10 inches square, contains the six tombs, in a row from east to west, the tombs themselves, of course, lying north and south. In the middle of each of its four sides, is a doorway, and on either side of each of these is a fanlight window. These are beautiful specimens of perforated stone-work. The whole window is filled with interlaced Arabic writing, and the perforations are the blank spaces in and around the letters. They let in a subdued light to the interior, which, with that of the open doors, is just sufficient to reveal a most remarkable flat stone ceiling. Almost every building of note in Bijapur has some remarkable feature peculiar to itself, either in constructive skill or decoration. This inner ceiling was the *chef d'œuvre*

* The tombs of men and women are easily known the one from the other. Those of the former have a long arched ridge along the top, which slopes slightly from north to south, while those of the latter have perfectly flat tops. The body is laid in the grave with the head to the north, and lying on the right side with the face towards Makka.

of the architect of the Ibrahim Rauza. It is simply a hanging ceiling. The whole span is the breadth of the room, viz., 39 feet 10 inches, of which a margin of 7 feet 7 inches broad, all round, curves upwards and inwards to a perfectly flat surface in the centre 24 feet square. Upon closely examining this, it is found to be composed of slabs of stone set edge to edge, with no apparent support. There are certainly two deep ribs, or beams, across both ways, but these are decorative and are made up of separate stones, and do not, in any way, support the slabs in the nine bays into which they divide the ceiling. This has been a most daring piece of work, carried out in defiance of the ordinary rules and regulations for the construction of buildings. But the architect not only foresaw exactly what he wanted, and how to accomplish it, but he had that thorough confidence in his materials, without which no builder ever yet produced anything that was lasting. It is a common thing to hear those, who think themselves able to judge, condemning the workmanship of the buildings of Bijapur ; and, certainly, when the rules and specifications of building, as they now hold in this country, are applied to these works, they are found constantly erring. These old Bijapur buildings have stood the best test any could stand, that of time, and the result proves amply that their builders knew what they were about. There were, probably, no contractors or middle-men in those days ; defrauding the state would have been punished with death. South of the walls of the town, there is half a dome, a good deal overhanging, which has thus remained since it was partly shot away by a cannon ball in the seige under Aurangzib, two hundred and twenty years ago! The whole secret of the durability of their masonry is the great strength and tenacity of its mortar. This is the secret, too, of this flat ceiling. At the north-east corner of the Taj Bauri is a partly destroyed dome. It is rather flat, and is constructed in the same way as this ceiling, with a lining of great flat slabs, which, by themselves, could not possibly stand. But they are nothing more than the stone lining of a concrete ceiling, the sheer adhesive strength of the mortar keeping them in position. It is possible, as is seen in the upstair corridor of the tomb, that, although the ceiling, as a whole, may remain intact, yet there is the danger of individual stones dropping out, and this is guarded against by rabbetting the edges, and, in many cases, fastening adjacent stones with iron clamps. The ceilings of the corridors are supported in the same way, and they may all be examined from below and above, staircases leading to the upper chambers through the thickness of the walls from behind the east and west doorways.

The exterior of the sepulchral chamber is most elaborately decorated with shallow surface tracery of arabesque and beautifully interlaced extracts from the Quran. The effect has been further enhanced by colour, but, unfortunately, this has weathered badly; still a little cleaning and varnishing would bring out the most of it. The doors are of teak, are carved in the panels with Arabic writing, and are furnished with deep carved cross bars carrying gilt iron bosses. The pillars in the corridors are very Hindu in style, and have little that is Saracenic about them. The ceiling of the inner verandah is worked all over with shallow surface carving into geometric, lotus, key, spiral, and intricate knot patterns. The arches in the outer verandah are additions, made some years ago, when the whole fabric was put in repair.

An inscription over the door says —

"Heaven stood astonished at the elevation of this building, and it might be said, when its head rose from the earth, that another heaven was erected. The garden of Paradise has borrowed its beauty from this garden, and every column here is graceful as the cyprus tree in the garden of Purity. An angel from heaven announced the date of the structure by saying, 'This building, which makes the heart glad, is the memorial of Taj Sultana.'"

The last sentence gives the date A.H. 1036 (A.D. 1626). From the inscription it appears that the building was built as Taj Sultana's tomb, but her husband Ibrahim, dying before her, was buried in it.*

Above the flat ceiling, already described, is another empty chamber under the dome. Passages lead up to this from behind the east and west doors, and thence up on to the terrace around the base of the dome.

Both the tomb, and the mosque opposite to it, are noted for their deep rich cornices and graceful minarets. The amount of labour expended on these has been unstinted. Under the cornice of the mosque may be seen the remnants of heavy chains with pendants.

---

* The building, in old writings, is also called the tomb of Zohrah Sultana.

Each of these has been carved out of a single block of stone. Some beautiful specimens of this work may be seen at the celebrated tomb of a saint at Rauza, above the Elura Caves, near Aurangabad, and also on the Kala Masjid at Lakshmeshwar, in the Dharwar district, in which town they are still made. Altogether, this group is the most elaborately decorated in or around Bijapur. The perforated parapets, round the tops of the buildings, look, at a distance, like a fringe of lace. The grouping of the miniature *minars*, round the bases of the corner minarets, is very pleasing. An incription, near the south door of the tomb, says that Malik Sandal, the architect, expended 1,50,000 huns, or about £70,000 on the building.

The Adaulat Mahal.—The Adaulat Mahal, or Hall of Justice, is now the residence of the Collector, and is therefore private. There is nothing about it worth particular notice. It has been extensively rebuilt, and little of the original walls of the old ruin can be distinguished from the new work. Beside it, serving now as out houses, is what was once the Suraj Mahal, and beneath these are extensive underground apartments.

The Arash Mahal.—Like the last, this is also a converted building, and is now the Civil Surgeon's residence. It is on the east of the Adaulat Mahal. Standing out before it, on one of the bastions of the old citadel wall, are the remains of a small pavilion. This was originally a little garden or pleasure house, and beneath it ran the moat which divided it from the plain without the walls. It was probably here that the king sat and watched military manœuvres and reviews of his troops, which are said to have taken place on this plain. The front, judging from the grooves in the masonry for woodwork, was evidently hung with curtains, while behind, are traces of brick work where a cook room appears to have been, and where, in the middle of the floor, is let in a hollow stone for husking rice or pounding curry stuff. The walls are covered with very clean cut surface ornament, in which are represented plates with melons and other fruits and wine bottles. There are a number of inscriptions also. One of these tells us that, "On this bastion is built the mansion of pleasure." Another gives the name of Ali II., viz., Abul Muzaffar Padshah Ali Adili. A third gives the date A.H. 1080 (A.D. 1669.) A fourth says, "The writing was written by the slave of the palace, Taqi Alhusaini, in A.H. 1081." A fifth has the Shiah declaration that Ali was the Vicar of Allah. A sixth tells us these verses (or houses?) were composed (or built?) by His Majesty Ali Adil Shah Ghazi. The masonry of these walls is particularly good, and bears a striking resemblance to that of the little Makka mosque.

The Anand Mahal.—This is another converted building. It is the most conspicuous palace in the citadel, and has a particularly fine large open hall. It has been made into a residence for the First Assistant Collector. The façade was never finished, it having been the intention of the builders to continue the arching further along on both sides of the present three arches. The appearance of the building has suffered considerably from the new additions. It was built by Ibrahim II. in A.D. 1589. It is difficult to say which was the finer palace of the two, this or the Gagan Mahal beside it. The Anand Mahal, or Palace of Delight, was probably the king's residence, containing his private apartments, while the Gagan Mahal was the great Durbar Hall. Immediately behind the palace are some small buildings, the nearest being a little plain mosque with two inscriptions in its *mehrab*. The next room to this is the station library.

The Gagan Mahal.—The Gagan Mahal, or Hall of Audience, a little to the west of the last, is remarkable for the immense arch which, with two tall narrow ones flanking it, forms its façade. It is said to have been built by Ali (I.) Adil Shah in 1561, and originally served the twofold purpose of a royal residence and Durbar Hall, where state business was transacted. The private apartments were above the great Hall of Audience, and were supported in front by two massive wooden pillars. Above these pillars were probably galleries, from which the ladies of the royal household could, through the suspended screens, see what was going on below. Staircases ascend to these upper apartments through the thickness of the back wall, and one stairway descends to the outhouses and kitchens on the west of the building.

The façade now stands out alone from the rest of the building, to which it was originally connected by cross arches and flat vaulted roofing. In the Sangat Mahal at Torveh, four miles out to the west of Bijapur, we have a duplicate of this building, though not so large, the roof of which is, in part, remaining. From this may be seen the manner in which this building was covered in. All the timber work, which must have been very valuable, was cleared away by the Marathas.

The main feature of this palace is its great central arch, which has a span of 60 feet 9 inches. It was desirable, of course, to have a clear open front before the Darbar Hall, unobstructed by piers or masonry of any kind, so that the king and his nobles could have an uninterrupted view of the assemblage without, and also witness tournaments and duels that appear to have taken place on the sward before the hall. To accomplish this, the architect decided that his span should be equal to the length of the front of the hall. But, unfortunately, the result is not pleasing. He forgot to take into account the height of the building, when determining upon the span, and the result is an unwieldy arch, out of all good proportion, and much too low for its width. Many a stirring scene took place here, and, it is said, that, in this hall, Aurangzib received the submission of the king Sikandar and his nobles on the fall of Bijapur.

The Sat Manjli.—The pile of apartments known as the Sat Manjli or Seven Storeys, stands a little way to the south-west of the Gagan Mahal, at the corner of a range of buildings, enclosing a quadrangle, and called the Granary. At present it rises to a height of five storeys, 97 feet over all, but a narrow stair rises from the fifth to a sixth which does not now exist. It is possible there may have been one still higher terrace, though very small, above this again. It was said to have been built by Ibrahim II. in 1583 as a palace, but, if so, it must have been far more extensive than it is at present, for its accommodation is very limited. It certainly extended a little way further on the south side, and still further along the walls on the north. One peculiar feature of this class of buildings is the amount of water pipes and cisterns about them, such as are found at Mubarak Khan's Mahal in the south-east of the city, and the water pavilions at Kumatgi. Here we have cisterns on the different floors, and, like the Kumatgi and Mubarak Khan's pavilions, the walls were subsequently painted with figures and other ornament. Traces of two of the figures still remain on the north wall of the first floor, and the imaginative mind has detected in them the outlines of the portrait of Rhumba, the favourite of Muhammad, and the Sultan himself. The walls are said to have been beautifully gilded, until the Rajah of Satara ordered it to be scraped off, thinking thereby to reap a rich harvest of the precious metal. As with the Gagan Mahal, all the wood-work has been carried away. It is, certainly, by no means a handsome looking building now, but there is no doubt that the richly carved window screens and weather boards, when they existed, improved it much. The building would seem to have been erected as a pleasure house wherein to spend an idle hour, and from the higher storeys of which to sit and watch what might be going on in the city or in the country around, in fact a royal watch tower. This was a very necessary thing in those days, when the king's life was never safe from the evil machinations of intriguing ministers who could surround the palace or citadel with his troops before the inmates were aware of it.

Immediately in front of the Sat Manjli is a neat little structure, standing alone, the use of which is not very apparent. It was probably a water pavilion, standing in the middle of a reservoir which has since been filled up. Its finish and general workmanship remind one of the little pavilion in front of the Arash Mahal. The Hindus have a belief among them that it is a *rath* or sacred car, having its wheels buried in the ground below. There is a very similar edifice, though not quite so fine, and which is falling into decay, in the fields, a short distance to south-east of Mustafa Khan's mosque.

From the top of the Sat Manjli a very fine view of the city and surrounding country may be obtained. Commencing with the buildings on the north, and going round the compass, we have, among the trees in the near middle distance, the minarets and dome of the little Bukhara Masjid, by the Post Office, while, a little further to the right, is the unfinished arched façade of the Ali (I.) Rauza. Immediately below us is part of the citadel moat, and straight above its far end, in the distance, rise the towers of the Bahmani Gate. Further to the right, or east-ward, and close under us, is the bare back wall of the Gagan Mahal with one of its front arches appearing at one side, and the tennis courts before it. Partly covered by it, and further away, is the Adaulat Mahal or Collector's residence, below which, and nearer to us, is the little building which has been converted into the station church. To the right of the Adaulat Mahal is the Arash Mahal, the residence of the Civil Surgeon, which is partly covered by the larger building, the Anand Mahal, the residence of the Assistant Collector. Behind this, and connected with it by a flying arch, is the station library. Right above the Anand Mahal, in the distance, rises the Ali Burj, upon which is a large iron gun. To the right of the Anand Mahal is the Gol Gumbaz with its great dome, while, close under it, is the white dome of of Hasham Pir.

Due east, in the middle distance, is the back wall of the Asar Mahal, with a row of small lancet openings along its top, and immediately below it, is a line of arches and the ruins of buildings on the citadel wall. Above all these, in the far away distance, on the plain beyond the city, may be seen the black mass of the unfinished tomb of Jahan Begam at Ainapur. Further to the right, and in line with the Asar Mahal, are two domes, close beside one another, the first, and smaller, belonging to the Chinch Diddi mosque, built upon the citadel walls, while the next, and larger one, is the dome of Mustafa Khan's mosque. Immediately below this, standing up out of the high walled enclosure around it, is one of the heavy looking towers of the Makka mosque, the other being hidden behind a large tree. Below this again, and much closer to us, are the ruins of a building which has been erroneously called the old mint. Still further round to the right, above the top of the crenelated wall of the citadel, is the dome of the Jami Masjid, and, beyond this, are the two minarets and upper portion of the city walls in the distance above it. South-east, and closer to us, are the bastions around the old citadel gate, and, below this, again, is the old mosque of Malik Karim-u-din, with the centre of its roof raised on small pillars above the rest. Coming round more to the south, we see, on the horizon, the Ibrahimpur Mosque, while, below it, and a little further round, is the tall Andu Masjid with its ribbed dome and group of little *minars*. Further on still, in the middle distance, is the Chota Chini Mahal, converted into a residence for the Superintendent of Police, and, immediately above it, is the Landa Kasab bastion, upon which is the largest gun in Bijapur. Below all these, and at our feet, is the range of buildings called the Chini Mahal, now converted into public offices.

Due south, is a short length of well built crenelated wall—a repaired portion of the city walls. Round more to the south-west, we pass Ibrahim's old Jami Masjid, with its partly ruined brick minarets, and, beyond this, almost covered by trees, is the Ali (I.) Rauza. Then comes, in the distance, the dome of Pir Shekh Hamid Qadri's tomb, with the incomplete tomb of Kishwar Khan down below it. To the right of the last, is the large enclosure of the Begam Sahiba's Rauza, where Aurangzib's wife is said to have been buried. Now follow the "Two Sisters," so named from the similarity and close proximity of their two domes. Immediately on the right of these, but in the far distance, is the square tomb of Haidar Khan.

In a straight line west of us, are the dome and minarets of the Ibrahim Rauza, the mosque being exactly covered by the tomb. Beyond it is seen the white dome of the Moti Dargah. Close down below us, to the right, at the cross-roads, is Jahan Begam's mosque. Further away, again, may be seen the red roof of the station hospital, and to the right of it the white walls of Aurangzib's Idgah, now the police lines. To the north-west, and nearer, is the clumsy looking Dekhani Idgah with the lofty Haidar Burj beside it, and, beyond them, in the distance, is the white dome of the Amin Dargah. This completes the circle.

The Granary.—The great quadrangle, together with the Chini Mahal at its south end, of which the Sat Manjli forms the north-west corner, has been known as the Granary. There is nothing about these buildings, whatever, to lead one to believe they were once a Granary. The Chini Mahal, called so from the amount of broken china found about there, was, at one time, a very fine building. It had a great lofty open verandah in front, and, in this respect, was somewhat similar to the Gagan Mahal. Within is a splendid hall, 128 feet long, by 29 feet broad, rising to the roof of the building, and flanked with suites of rooms on different levels. Here, again, the staircases lead up through the back wall. It is very difficult to say what the building was originally intended for, but it has been turned to account of late years, and is now the location of the public offices of the Collectorate. All round the quadrangle was an arcade, which has also been converted, and is now used as record rooms, etc. There is no doubt that this arcade was used by the household troops who lived in the open verandahs and tethered their horses to the basement, as is usual in the houses of chiefs at the present day. The discovery of grain, in quantities, used for the horses' food, probably led to the idea of the place having been a granary. It was at the excavations, carried on here, that the beautiful wrought iron screen was found which now stands in the little church beside the Gagan Mahal.

The Makka Masjid.—This is an exceedingly neat little mosque, shut in between great high walls. The towers or minarets, from which the call to prayer was cried, are, without doubt, the only remaining portions of a very early mosque. On the east side of the enclosure, is buried a Pir or saint, who is said to have built a mosque here about the end of the thirteenth century. It is very likely that this was so, and that the towers are the remnants of it. It was only after the inroads of Malik Kafur, in the beginning of the fourteenth century, that the Muhammadans became sufficiently masters of the country to break up, with impunity, old Hindu temples for materials with which to construct their mosques; before this time, the few Muhammadans who had penetrated into these districts were here on sufferance, and, if they wished to build, they had to obtain their own material. So we find, from these towers, that they were constructed with rough material and apparently unskilled labour. It is, indeed, very difficult to say with what object the great high walls were built which partly encompass this mosque. It is certain they were not intended for defence of any kind, for the four great arched openings in the south face have never been provided with doors, nor has any arrangement, in the masonry jambs, been provided for their subsequent insertion. The uniform distances of these arches from the end, shew that it was intended to completely enclose the rectangular space, which work was stopped by the presence of the towers, and, perhaps, the old mosque to which they belonged. On examining the end and north walls, we find great square holes knocked through the masonry in a line, at a good height above the ground, which were apparently intended to receive the ends of beams that supported the roof of a shed of some kind. The only suggestion I can make, is that this great enclosure was intended for, and the west end actually used as, elephant stables. The high wall was intended to shelter the animals from the heat of the sun, as well as to shut off the noise and smell from the adjacent palace buildings, and the arches, each large enough to allow an elephant, with his keeper on his back, to pass under freely, are all on the south side, *i.e.*, furthest away from the palaces and other buildings. This idea receives further confirmation from the fact that, just outside this enclosure, on the south, and almost touching its walls, is a tower, called the Bijjanhalli or Bichkanhalli tower,* which, on close inspection, turns out to be a storehouse for grain or food of some kind. It was roofed over, as may be seen from inside, where the slots, in the top of the wall, shew where the roof timbers were let in, and covered with eight or ten inches of concrete. Outside are the plaster drains down the sides to carry off the rain from the roof, such as exist down the west face of the Sat Manjli. A doorway was made on the north side, near the high wall, and steps lead up the outside to the top. These last arrangements are similar to those of Muhammad Shah's granary, near the Jami Masjid, where steps lead up to the roof, by which grain was carried up and poured into the rooms below, through holes in the roof, and was drawn off as required from the doorways.

It is not unlikely that, when these walls were built, the old mosque was in ruins, and it was intended to remove it and complete the enclosure, but that, at this juncture, some Qazi probably interfered, and explained how impious an act it would be to remove a mosque when once built, and use the sanctified ground for other purposes.† It was then just left as it was, and the west end used as

---

* This tower has been supposed to be the old watchtower of the village of Bijjanhalli, which village existed somewhere in this neighbourhood before Bijapur became a city.

† Read the story in connection with the building of the Kanathi Masjid in the Itinerary after "Jami Masjid."

elephant stables; subsequently the mosque was rebuilt as we see it now. The two old towers of the former mosque were then included in the angles of the corridors of the new one, and their staircases repaired, or rather rebuilt with stone, as far as the roof of the corridor. Beyond that they were not required, and the old brick and wood ones were left as they were. The new mosque is said to have been built for the use of the ladies of the royal household, which accounts for it being placed within this enclosure. In the ordinary mosques, used by the men, there is a *mimbar* or pulpit, from which the address is given, but, in the women's mosque, this was not provided, for the simple reason that no man could be allowed in to give them an address. There is thus no *mimbar* in this mosque.

Old Mosque.—Not far from the south-east corner of the Chini Mahal is one of the earliest mosques in Bijapur. It is wholly made up of pillars, beams, and cornices, taken from older Hindu shrines. The porch, in fact, is part of a Hindu temple *in situ*; it is the hall or *mandap*, with its pillars and niches, but wanting part of its roof. The shrine, which was built on to this hall on the west, has been entirely cleared away, and a through passage thus gained to the courtyard within. The inner doorway, with perforated screen panels on either side of it, has been inserted by the Muhammadans. This space, between it and the next opening, was the antechamber to the shrine of the original temple. An examination of the ends of the walls will shew how the shrine has been broken away from the rest.

Across the west side of the courtyard, is the mosque, made up of pillars of all patterns and heights, brought to one uniform level with odd pieces, and, over these, are laid the cross beams and slabs forming the roof. An inscription, on a pilaster inside, tells us that Malik Karim-u-din erected the upper part of the mosque in A.D. 1320, and that Revoya, a carpenter of Salhaodage, carried out the work. Karim-u-din was the son of Malik Kafur, the general of Alla-u-din, who conducted several successive campaigns against the Hindu kingdoms of the south. The central portion of the mosque has been raised by pillars, perched upon the lower ones, thus admitting more light and air into the body of the building. This construction is similar to that carried out in the Ahmedabad and Gujarat mosques, and is the only example in that style in Bijapur. In the courtyard is a mound which is said to be the place of burial of several Muhammadans who fell in a *melee* with the Hindus when the former first settled here. Another old mosque, built of Hindu pillars, stands in the grounds of the Adaulat Mahal, with its back to the road which passes north and south through the Arkilla.

The Citadel Gateway.—The only gateway left to the citadel is that on the south, the exit facing east. Approaching it from the east, the roadway doubles round an outstanding covering wall, furnished with a corner bartizan or watch turret, into the space before the outer main gate. On the wall to the left of this turret is an inscription containing the profession of faith and then the words, "Door-work of Kurda Khan Jita Gujarati, in the year 951" (A.D. 1544). Over the outer gate is a long inscription consisting of an invocation to Ali. Passing in through this, we enter the space between the inner and outer gates. On either side of the latter, within, are arcades which served as guardrooms. High up on the bastion to the right are two inscriptions; one says that the bastion was called the Elahi or Divine Bastion and that it was built in the time of Ibrahim I., in A.H. 945 (A.D. 1538), while the other is an invocation to Ali with good wishes for the king Adil Shah.

Before us stands the skeleton of the inner gate, nearly the whole of it having disappeared; two uprights and a great cross beam being all that is now left to represent it. Built into the wall, low down on the south side of this, is a beautifully inscribed slab in the old Kanarese character, which will be noticed further on in the historical account. Just inside this gateway are the remains of other guardrooms, constructed entirely of pillars from Hindu temples.* The majority of these pillars are of a later date than those

* From the fact that several of these pillars have cross lines roughly scratched upon them, upon which to play games somewhat akin to draughts, it is evident that they must have been lying prone upon the ground for some considerable time before being used here. It rather favours the idea that they were not rifled from standing temples but had been found lying about. If the pillars had been taken from standing temples, the despoilers would have found the capitals there to match, which would have saved them much trouble in piecing and patching, afterwards, to get them to an uniform height.

used in the old mosque of Malik Karim, and belong, principally, to the Vijayanagar period.

On a turret on the walls, further along to the west, behind the Chini Mahal, is an inscription which tells us that Muhah Harbakzah built the citadel here in the time of Abu-l-Muzaffar Adil Shah. The walls and bastions, around the gateway, and for some distance on both sides of it, are further strengthened by outer works. There was probably a drawbridge or some similar contrivance before the gateway spanning the moat.

The Andu Masjid.—The mosque, known by the name of the Andu Masjid,* stands on the east side of the road running from the citadel to the Landa Kasab bastion, and not far from the former. It is a two-storeyed building, but not a two storeyed mosque. The mosque occupies the upper floor only, the lower or ground floor being a hall or rest house. The reason for placing this mosque upon the second storey is not apparent; it was perhaps a whim and nothing more. A long inscription, above the entrance doorway below, tells us the mosque was built by I'tbar Khan in A.D. 1608.† He was one of the ministers of Ibrahim I. The excessive hyperbole, in which Muhammadan chroniclers delighted to indulge, is well illustrated in this inscription, where it says, "At the sight of the elevation of this cupola, the cupola of the sky is in lamentation" from grief at the rivalry. And "the architect of this paradise-like mosque is His Excellency I'tbar Khan. One has seen

* On account of its egg-shaped dome.

† His tomb is outside the city, near the Ibrahim Rauza.

few mosques of this fashion ; a fashion of this kind is heart-ravishing."

This mosque is about the best built of any in Bijapur, the surface of the stone is all but polished; the joints of the masonry are so fine that the edge of a sheet of note paper could barely be inserted between them ; and the weathering of three hundred years seems hardly to have left its impress upon it. The ornament is sparingly and discreetly applied, and its general appearance is greatly enhanced by the numerous off-sets and recessed angles in the perpendicular lines. The front seems not to have been quite finished, the two large lower brackets, under the cornice, one on the face of each pier, have not been inserted, but the corbels and slots have been made for them. Some of the bands of ornament about the *mehrab* are also unfinished. Around the inside walls is a pretty horizontal string course of *pan* or leaf ornament.

The mosque occupies the west side of the roof of the lower storey, the east side being a terrace before it. Stairways lead down, through the walls, from the two outer corners of the terrace. The dome is of the ribbed melon-shape variety which occurs in two or three instances in Bijapur, and the bulbs or tops of the *minars* are also ribbed. These *minars* rise from each of the four corners, and in an additional group of four above the *mehrab* buttress at the back of the dome. With the ribbed dome rising between them, and the little *minars* round the bases of the larger ones, the effect from a little distance is very pleasing. A handsome perforated parapet, forming a lace-like fringe, adorns the crest of the building. A plain horizontal string course, on the outside of the walls, shews the line of meeting of the upper and lower storeys, and, while the upper is very ornate, the lower is severely plain. The ground floor was evidently intended as a rest house for travellers.

The only two-storeyed mosque in, or about, Bijapur is that connected with the cenotaph of Afzal Khan, some distance to the west of the city, and a short way beyond Afzalpur.

The Landa Kasab Gun and Bastion.—The Landa Kasab bastion is one of those in the south wall of the city, some distance to the west of the Fateh gate; the road leads to it direct from the Andu Masjid. It is the second bastion on the left at the end of this road. There is nothing remarkable in the bastion itself, but, upon it, rests the largest piece of ordnance in Bijapur. This great gun measures 21 feet 7 inches long, diameter at the breech 4 feet 4 inches, at the muzzle 4 feet 5 inches, calibre 1 foot 7½ inches, length of bore 18 feet 7½ inches, and estimated weight, nearly 47 tons. It is constructed in the same manner as the guns on the Haidar Burj already described. Beside this gun is a smaller one of most unusual dimensions which looks like another big gun cut down, but it was probably an attempt at a mortar.

A little distance away to the south-east from this bastion, are seen some mounds, which are supposed to be the position where Aurangzib posted his battery when he breached the walls on this side. This particular bastion shews many shot marks, one ball having struck the muzzle of the big gun, upon which it has left its impression.

Upon the bastion is an inscription which records its erection during the time of Ali I.

Shah Karim Muhammad Qadri's Tomb.—This, with that of Sayyid Abdul Rehman Qadri, is situated near the south-east corner of the courtyard of the Jami Masjid. They both have ceilings which are said to have been coated with a wash of pulverised mother-of-pearl, giving them a silvery sheen; and the second tomb has also some very pretty raised stucco work in the ceiling. Over the doorway of Shah Karim's tomb, which is the better cared for, is an inscription which says "The wonderful *dargah*, blessed, solid, upright, has become a delightful spot of pilgrimage for disciples. The following date came according to the mode of believers, 'The world (or, the scholar?) is in the shadow of this cupola of Shah Karim.'" This last sentence gives the date 1741. There are some neat iron bosses on the doors of this tomb.

Mustafa Khan's Mosque and Palace.—About five hundred yards east of the citadel, are the mosque and palace of Mustafa Khan. The mosque is a very lofty, substantially built, edifice. The front has three tall arches, the central one being very much wider than the side ones, and, being almost devoid of ornament, the façade has rather a bald appearance. A deep heavy cornice overhangs the front, and the octagonal buttresses which were to carry minarets, flank the front of the building. The minarets have never been built. The large dome is stilted by the introduction, between it and the roof, as in the Jami Mosque, of a second storey, with a row of arched recesses on each face.

The cross arches, inside, divide the ceiling into three bays. The central bay is worked up, by pendentives, to a fourteen-sided figure, and, from this, rises the dome. The side bays are wagon-vaulted. Although the mosque is so lofty, yet its effect is much spoiled by the want of elevation in the springing lines of the arches,—the piers are too short.

Behind the mosque, to the west, are the ruins of Mustafa Khan's Palace. Judging from the extent of the different blocks of building, courtyards, gateways, tanks, and gardens, it must have been an extensive residence. In the garden, around the large tank, may be seen lengths of shallow channels, with serrated beds, down which the overflow of the tank was allowed to run in thousands of little ripples.

Mustafa Khan Ardistani was, at first, in the service of Ibrahim Kutb Shah of Golkonda, and was the emissary and agent who conducted the arrangements between the kings of Golkonda, Bidar, Bijapur, and Ahmednagar which led to the great victory of Talikot and destruction of Vijayanagar. After this, he entered the service of the Bijapur king, and his career and murder are described further on in the historical outline of the Adil Shahis.

The mosque is also called the Ek-chip-ka-masjid, on account of a very small piece of stone—a "chip"—being built into the masonry in its south-west corner.

The Bari Kaman.—Not far to the south of Mustafa Khan's mosque, and spanning the road leading to the latter, is a great archway which appears to have been the entrance to the grounds of his palace. There is nothing particularly worthy of notice about it except its size.

Ali Shahid Pir's Mosque.—This is a small, but very peculiar mosque, in the fields to the south of the Mehtar Mahal. Its peculiarity lies in the singular wagon-vaulted roof which covers the whole mosque, and which, with the exception of a smaller and more rudely constructed mosque to the west of this one, is not found elsewhere in Bijapur. The wagon-vault occurs, often enough, as roofing for a single small bay of a ceiling, where the principal bays are domed, but not, except in these cases, as one vaulted roof covering the entire mosque. In the smaller specimens, it is a more or less flat vault without a central ridge line, whereas, in this masjid, it has a very great rise, and a central ridge line running across the whole width of the building. The end walls rise vertically to meet the vault and do not, like the smaller examples, arch into it. Two transverse arches, slightly projecting from the surface, divide the vaulted ceiling into three sections, and these are further subdivided, by vertical and horizontal ribs, into small panels.

The façade of this mosque is very pleasing, from the effect gained by introducing a great number of receding lines of moulding round the arches, giving them a deep-set appearance; and these lines are carried down the piers.

The outer ring of arch moulding is cusped, and the spandrels are ornamented with beautifully designed medallions in stucco. There are short thin minarets, one at each end of the façade, and, over the *mehrab*, is a dome whose top rises above the ridge of the roof. A curious thing, in connection with the *mehrab*, is the presence of a little doorway inserted in one side of it, thus giving access to it from the outside of the mosque. This is very unusual.

Over the *mehrab* is an inscription in coloured enamel. The letters are white on a blue ground. This is surrounded by a border composed of two yellow bands, between which, is a row of flowers, yellow and white alternately, each separated by a vertical green bar on a dark blue ground. The inscription contains verses from the Quran only. The whole front of the *mehrab* was covered with inlaid encaustic tiles, but nearly all has been picked off and carried away. The inscription is perfect, but the border round it has commenced to suffer, and, if not better cared for, will certainly disappear altogether.

Beside the mosque is the insignificant looking tomb of Hazrat Sayyid Ali Shahid, after whom the mosque is named. He was killed in battle fighting against infidels, and hence became a *shahid* or martyr, and the mosque is said to have been built in his honour by Ali I.

Ibrahim's Jami Masjid.—This mosque is also known as Ali's old Jami Masjid, and also as the Datri-ki-masjid. It is situated about three hundred yards to the south-west of the Andu Masjid, in the fields. This is one of the old-fashioned mosques, of which there are a few in Bijapur, with brick and mortar minarets, not only over the corners of the building, but also over the central piers. Another mosque of this type is that of Ikhlas Khan near the Fateh Gate. The mosque is ascribed to Ibrahim I. and is said to have been built in A.H. 958 (A.D. 1551).

Ali (I.) Roza.—Two hundred and fifty yards south-west of the last building, is the tomb of Ali (I.) Adil Shah. It is an exceedingly plain structure. In plan it is a plain rectangular room surrounded by a corridor. The roofing of this inside room is rather peculiar, and is a good example of a style of vaulting carried out in several buildings in Bijapur. There are here four tombs,—one of a male adult, one of a female adult, and two of children. The exterior of the walls of this inner chamber has been painted, but it has so weathered that little of it can now be seen, but, if cleaned and varnished, it would be much improved. Over the north doorway are painted inscriptions containing the Shiah profession of faith, the throne verse, and the words "Allah and Muhammad apostle," but no name of king or date. We have nothing but tradition to fix upon this as the last resting place of Ali (I.) Adil Shah.

At the south-east corner of this building is a beautifully built, high, square, platform, upon the middle of which is a tombstone of well finished masonry. The sides of the platform are divided into panels with censers and chains in each, and at each corner is a projecting foot or support such as are seen under the corners of trays, and which are here intended to appear as supporting the platform. There is no other tombstone in Bijapur which is so neatly designed and carefully finished as this; and the nature of this close-grained dark green stone lends itself well to such work. No one knows whose tomb it is, tradition even being silent. This is a great pity, as it is, without doubt, the resting place of a person of rank.

Tomb of Pir Shekh Hamid Qadri.—This building, which stands close to the walls in the south-west corner of the city, nearly four hundred yards west of Ali (I.) Adil Shah's tomb, covers the remains of the saints Shekh Hamid Qadri and his brother Shekh Latif Ulla Qadri, who lived in Bijapur during the reign of Ibrahim II. A local MS. says the tomb was built by Fatimah Sultana, relict of Ali (I.) Adil Shah, and that these two men died in 1602 and 1612 respectively. In Fatimah's well close by, and which is generally called the Gumat *bauri*, just in front of the mosque attached to this tomb, is an inscription which says that in the saltanate of Shah Ali Adil Shah this "bairi" was constructed by Setti Fatimah Solmansetti in the year A.H. 970, *i.e.*, A.D. 1562. It is evident the same Fatimah is meant in both cases, so there must be some mistake about the first two dates, or she was an old lady when she had the tomb built.

Close beside this tomb is the mosque, and, before it, on the east, are two other tombs in line, one having a pyramidal roof, and said, on that account, to be the tomb of a Shiah.

This south-west corner of the city would seem, from the number of early buildings, tanks, and wells crowded into it, to have been the favourite quarter in times preceding the the reign of Ibrahim II., and was possibly laid out with gardens and terraces.

The Janjiri or Malika Jahan Begam's Mosque.—The building known as the Janjiri Masjid, or Malika Jahan Begam's mosque, is situated amongst the trees immediately to the west of the Sat Manjli, just outside the citadel walls. It is an exceedingly neat mosque, with a good, well proportioned cornice and a particularly rich façade. Of the three arches, in front, the central one is cusped; the cornice and its brackets are very prettily chased, and the outer edge of the former, being cut into scollops, it has the appearance of having a narrow edging of lace. Along the top of the building, between the minarets, has been a very ornamental perforated parapet, and, vertically above the piers of the arches, are little *chattris* or canopies with small tracery windows in each side of them. The minarets of the façade are very graceful, and are in good proportion; there are two others over the back corners of the mosque. Great pains have been taken in decorating the surfaces of the leaves round the neck of the dome, above the roof, with stucco ornament, but, unfortunately, the leaves are not high enough to be seen from below. This dome rises over the central bay before the *mehrab*, and the ceiling, within, is carried up the full height of the dome; in front of this is a very pretty ceiling with plaster ornament. The lines of the arch mouldings intersect very neatly on the piers. Before the mosque, in the platform, is a small square tank, now dry. There is no inscription in or about the mosque, but the building of it is ascribed to Ibrahim II., who is said to have built it in honour of his daughter Malika Jahan.

The Tombs of Khan Muhammad and Abdul Razaq Qadir.—These two tombs, the domes of which are very conspicuous objects, are known to European residents as the "Two Sisters," and to natives as the Jod Gumbaz, or pair of domes, on account of their close proximity and likeness, in size and shape, to one another. The octagonal building, on the south, is the resting place of the traitor Khan Muhammad, or Khan Khanam as his sovereign called him, and of his son Khawas Khan, Vazir to Sikandar. Khan Muhammad, who was in command of the troops in the field, was bought over by the commander of the imperial forces of Dehli, and remained inactive at a critical juncture, when he had the enemy entirely in his hands. Afzal Khan, who was in the field with him, thoroughly disgusted, withdrew and returned to Bijapur, and reported to the king how matters stood. Khan Muhammad was recalled, and, as he came into the city through the Makka gate, he was assassinated. Subsequently, Aurangzib gave instructions that the tax for one year, which Bijapur was now annually obliged to remit to Dehli, should be used for the building of a tomb over Khan Muhammad. Khawas Khan,* his son, Vazir to Sikandar,

* A title, merely, which several nobles held in succession.

was infected with the same treasonable impulses which possessed his father, and he, too, after being imprisoned at Bankapur, fell under the executioner's sword. His body was brought to Bijapur, and buried in the tomb of his father, which is thus generally called after him.

The larger square tomb is that of Abdul Razaq Qadir, Khawas Khan's religious tutor or "domestic chaplain," and was, no doubt, built at the same time as the other.

The floors of both tombs are at a very considerable elevation above the surrounding ground level, which is due to the vaults, containing the graves, being built upon the ground rather than beneath its surface, as is the case in most tombs. The tomb of Abdul Razaq Qadir is exceedingly plain, the square wall rising almost unbroken from the ground to the dome.

To the west of these two tombs is a third, which is said to be that of Sidi Rehan. Sidi Rehan Sholapuri was an officer of note who distinguished himself during the reign of Sultan Muhammad. It is alleged that he was purchased as a boy of seven years old, with his mother, by Ibrahim II. from a merchant at Nauraspur, and was sent to the palace to be the playmate of young prince Muhammad who was of the same age. One day the prince, in play, snatched the cap from Sidi Rehan's head and threw it into a tank. Sidi Rehan indignantly demanded his cap back, and complained to the king who had been looking on. The cap was brought, and the king, at the same time, prophesied that, when prince

Muhammad should become king, Sidi Rehan would be his minister.

Within Khawas Khan's tomb is one of the finest halls in Bijapur, unoccupied even by the usual counterfeit tombstones. This is unusual, and the absence of these has been taken to indicate that the hall was used as a dwelling. This was hardly so. As the tombs were built by Aurangzib, it is very likely he had ordered marble tombstones from northern India or elsewhere, such as are usual in Gujarat and Hindustān, but for some reason or other, they never reached Bijapur. He did precisely the same thing for his wife's tomb in the Nau Bag, and some of the marble slabs still lie in the lower rooms of the Asar Mahal.

This building was used, with the mosque attached, as an Executive Engineer's office and dwelling, but, owing to the great reverence with which the Muhammadans hold the memory of the saint Abdul Razaq, his tomb was not converted into a dwelling. These two tombs are the only other buildings, besides the Gol Gumbaz, that have galleries within the domes, but, owing to the small diameter of the latter, they have no distinct echo.

The Bukhara Masjid.—This stands close beside the Post Office. Little is known about the origin of the name given to it. It is a very neat little building, is carefully finished, and has a well designed cornice whose brackets are beautifully carved; there is some pretty stucco work about the arches within. The mosque has been, or was intended to be, enclosed within a courtyard, part of which, with its outer arcade and gateway, still stands before it.

Malik Sandal's Tomb and Mosque.—One hundred and fifty yards to the north-west of the last building is the group of buildings, known as Malik Sandal's tomb and mosque, with their surrounding arcades and walls. It is an exceedingly modest looking edifice for the last resting place of the greatest of Bijapur's architects, the man who carried out the construction of some of the finest buildings of the city.

Within the enclosed courtyard is a small canopy, beneath which is the tomb of a female, said to be that of the wife or mother of Malik Sandal, while, near it, are tombs in the open air, one of which is said to cover the remains of the great architect himself. In one corner of the courtyard is the mosque, a very primitive looking structure. The surrounding buildings contain rooms, arcades, and tanks, as if intended as a *sarai*, and, above these, are open terraces.

The small canopy, covering a tomb, and seen at a little distance to the north of this, with a ribbed egg-shaped dome, is called the the Kamrak-i-gumbaz.

Zamrud Masjid.—Close beside the end of the last group of buildings, on the south, is a miniature mosque only twelve feet square. It is well built, and is quite unique, in being the smallest mosque in Bijapur. About the *mehrab* are a number of Persian inscriptions containing extracts from the Quran.

The Chinch Diddi Mosque.—This is perched upon a bastion at the south-east corner of the citadel, and overlooks the Asar Mahal and the town round about the Jami Masjid. It is a very plain building, with little about it of interest save the remains of wall paintings within. These are very poor and weak, and have more the appearance of a common wall paper. The building known as Mubarak Khan's Mahal, already mentioned, was decorated in the same way, but neither is anything like the more solid looking wall painting at Kumatgi, described further on. This is evidently a late building; and, to make the bastion, which had been previously built, strong enough to carry it, the latter was further encased with an extra thickness of arched masonry, while a firmer foundation has been obtained, upon the top, by laying great heavy cross beams of wood under the foundations of the mosque.

The Chota Asar.—This is a small mosque, about two hundred and fifty yards to the east of the Dekhani Idgah, and remarkable for the abundance of rich ornament in stucco which covers the walls, ceiling, and part of the façade; otherwise there is nothing worth note about it. It has a very flat wagon-vaulted ceiling, a kind often met with in Bijapur, but nothing like that of Ali Shahid Pir's mosque. The manner in which the design is carried out on the walls is worth notice. Instead of forming the ornament, as it is elsewhere, in raised plaster on a flat surface, the workmen have here cut into the thick flat coating of plaster on the walls, and have removed that part of it which filled the interstices between the lines of the pattern. The consequence is that, although the design is in raised plaster yet it is on the same level as the general surface of the wall. This plaster work appears to have been further decorated with colour, but it is doubtful whether this addition was an improvement upon the uniform grey stucco with its delicate soft lights and shadows. It was certainly more gorgeous, but the pattern must have been somewhat obscured by it.

The Dekhani Idgah.—This is a most curious looking building, standing on the highest ground within the walls of Bijapur. An inscription, upon the face of it, says it was built by Malik (Sandal ?) during the reign of Ibrahim II. It is a very clumsy, ancient looking, building of no architectural merit whatever, and it is very unlikely that it was built during the time of Ibrahim. It was perhaps only repaired at that time, and was erected in the very early days of the Adil Shahis. Such an elevated spot of ground, within the walls, would never have remained unoccupied down to the time of Ibrahim II.

The Chand Bauri.—This large tank, the next *in importance to the Taj Bauri, is* situated in the north-west corner of the town, about one hundred and fifty yards south of the Shahapur gate. It is said to have been built by Ali (I.) Adil Shah in 1579 in honour of his Queen Chand Bibi, daughter of Husain Nizam Shah, the heroine of Meadows Taylor's "Noble Queen." This tank, no doubt, formed the model upon which the Taj Bauri was built. It is very much inferior to the latter in every way, but, like it, it has the arch spanning the steps which lead down to it, and a narrow ledge, round about it, taking the place of the terrace, with rooms on the south side.

Yaqut Dabuli's Mosque and Tomb.—These two buildings stand just outside the citadel, on the north-east, close to the roadway leading from the Collector's residence to the main road. The mosque, as it stands, is not the original edifice. The original is really encased within subsequent additions. It is the inner chamber. To this was added a wing on either side, forming side chambers, which were themselves divided, transversely, into a forward and a back room, the latter being entered from the back of the mosque. They were also divided into a lower and an upper storey. A further addition was the front hall with a three-arched façade and flat ceiling. The masonry of the additions is much better than that of the old mosque. The end walls of the forward addition are pierced with little narrow arched windows. These additions account for the number of minarets on the roof, there being the original ones and those of the later portions.

The tomb is a compact little square structure, with stone lattice work filling each of three sides, and the doorway on the south side. Inside, is a single tombstone over the grave of a male. Over the doorway is an inscription which says, "One atom of divine grace is better than to be chief of 1000 villages." And it also gives the name "Malik Yaqut Janata." His name occurs again in the inscription in the *mehrab* of the Jami Masjid. He was entrusted with the oversight of the decoration of the same.

Three hundred yards to the north-west, across the road, is the Yaqut Mahal, now converted into a Travellers' Bungalow, so that little of the original palace can be made out.

The Amin Dargah.—This tomb stands on the crest of a hill about two miles beyond the Shahapur gate. Its whitewashed dome is seen for several miles around. The road to it passes the Jail, which was originally a very extensive *sarai*, or resting place for travellers, built by Abul Bari Muhammed Mustafa Khan Sari in 1640. There is nothing particularly interesting about this tomb or those around it, but it is a pleasant trip out to it, which is well repaid by the fine views obtained of the country round from the hill top. Hazrat Khawjah Amin-ul-din, a Bijapur saint, was the son of Shah Burhan-ul-din. He died in 1664, and his tomb is said to have been built in 1675 by Afzal Khan Vazir.

For miles round this, the country is dotted over with mosques, tombs, and *sarais*; and, judging from the extensive ruins of foundations and walls in the immediate vicinity of Shahapur, there must have existed a very large suburb here at one time. Beyond Shahapur is the site of the great Ramling tank, the masonry dam of which, though much ruined, still exists. This is a pretty spot, the stream, running down the middle of it, being overshadowed with palms and other trees.

Afzal Khan's Cenotaph, Mosque, and Palace.—About a mile south-west of Shahapur and the Amin Dargah is the village of Afzalpur or Takki, in which, on the highest ground, is the tomb of Chindgi Shah, and, half a mile west of this again, is the cenotaph of Afzal Khan. Afzal Khan's story is told in the historical outline of the Adil Shahis further on. During his life he constructed his own tomb, with its attendant mosque, beside his palace, and appears to have finished the mosque in 1653. In the *mehrab*, of the same, is the date with his name. The tomb appears never to have been finished and was, no doubt, still in course of construction when he was ordered away on that fatal expedition against the treacherous Sivaji. The astrologers told him he would never return, and, so impressed was he by their predictions, that he set his house in order accordingly, put up the date of that year in his cenotaph, and is said to have drowned his sixty-four wives. He was killed really one month after the year expired ; but, when he left Bijapur for good, he was, to all intents and purposes, dead to it and his friends. His bones lie buried near the spot where he he was killed, on the slopes of Partabgarh, and were never brought back to be interred in his own tomb. Consequently the central unpaved space is unoccupied, but two women have been buried within the chamber.

Close to the tomb, and separated from it by a small cistern, is the mosque. This is peculiar, inasmuch as it is the only two-storeyed mosque in or around Bijapur. It is very probable that the upper floor was reserved for the women of the zanana, just, as in Ahmadabad, we find portions divided off, in most of the mosques, for their particular use.

Beside the cenotaph and mosque, on the south, are the ruins of his palace.

Some distance to the south-west of this, in a grove of trees, is a platform with the remains of a large tank* before it. On the former are eleven rows of tombs, all of them the tombs of females, amounting, in all, to sixty-three, with an unoccupied space which would have made the sixty-fourth. They are so regularly placed at equal intervals, and all so much alike as regards size and design, that it really looks as if the story, of Afzal Khan having drowned his wives, were true. They are pointed out as the tombs of Afzal Khan's wives. The story tells us that one or two escaped, and the vacant grave certainly seems to corroborate this statement. Perhaps the graves have suggested the story.

About two hundred and fifty yards east of this is the Surang Bauri, from which the great tunnel starts, which is said to have carried water into Bijapur, and which can be traced as far as the Ibrahim Rauza by its air shafts, which rise to the surface at frequent intervals along its route. The mouth of the tunnel may be seen in the *bauri* or well.

Nauraspur.—It is recorded that Ibrahim II., in 1599, determined to found a new city, which, in splendour, was to outshine all other cities. He summoned masons and artizans from all quarters, and placed Nawab Shavaz Khan in charge of the work. Twenty thousand workmen are said to have been engaged. Nobles, ministers, and rich merchants were induced to build, and, it is said, each vied with the other in trying to produce a residence better than his neighbour's; thus many fine *mahals* were erected and adorned with gilding and other decoration. Tradition says the astrologers

* Called by the people the "Muhammad Sarowar."

interfered and declared that evil would come upon the kingdom if the capital was removed to the new position, and it was then abandoned. The more correct account of the desertion of Nauraspur is rather different. In 1624, when Ibrahim was at war with Nizam Shah, the latter sent an army under Malik Ambar against Bijapur. As the walls of Nauraspur were not finished, Ibrahim withdrew to Bijapur, and left the new city to the mercy of the enemy. Malik Ambar, finding it unprotected, entered it, and completely wrecked it. Malik Ambar died in the following year, before Ibrahim had a chance of wreaking his vengeance upon him.

We have, left to us, the ruins of the great wall* of this city, surrounding more than half the circuit of the selected site, from which it may be seen that the new city, if completed, would have been more than half as large again as Bijapur. About the centre of this, near the village of Torveh, within a high walled enclosure, are the remains of the Nauras or Sangat Mahal, and, beside it, is the Nari Mahal. Beyond these are the Tagani Mahal and other mosques, tombs, and buildings of sorts.

It is related that, when the city was being laid out, a man from Torveh brought a vessel full of wine and presented it to king Ibrahim, who was so pleased with its delicious taste and fragrance, that he exclaimed, "To-day I have had a new enjoyment," using the word *naurasida*, meaning "newly obtained."

---

* The outer wall, or casing, only, is built, the earthen ramp and inner retaining wall had not been added.

These words are said to have been looked upon as very auspicious, and the city was called, on that account, Nauraspur. Another derivation of the name is *nau*, "new," *ras*, "juice" or "wine," and *pur*, a city, *i.e.*, the city of the new wine. But it is perhaps more likely to have been from *nauras*, "newly obtained" or "newly founded"—*nau* and *rasidan* "to obtain"—but having no connection with the wine story, and simply meaning "the new city." It is also called Naurozpur, from the festival of the Nauroz.

The Sangat Mahal is a duplicate, on a slightly smaller scale, of the Gagan Mahal in the citadel at Bijapur. It is in ruins, having suffered like the other buildings which originally had much woodwork about them. It is a lonely but picturesque spot, surrounded by cultivated plots of ground, forests of prickly pear, and heaps of ruins.

There appears to have been, at one time, a great broad road running straight from this towards Bijapur, known, now, as the Grand Bazar of Muhammad Shah. It can be distinctly traced for some distance, from near the Sangat Mahal to the Moti Gumbaz.

The headworks of the Torveh waterworks are at a point near the walls to the south-west of Torveh village, where a dam has been thrown across the course of a small stream which runs down the middle of a broad valley. Thence a small masonry tunnel runs towards Torveh village, and is then lost. Then, from the Sangat Mahal, a pipe is traced to a point over a mile to the north-east, where it turns south-east towards the Surang Bauri. From the Surang Bauri runs, towards Bijapur, the great Torveh tunnel. There is, or was, a very large tank, or lake, south of the Torveh road, from which a ruined aqueduct may be seen running in the direction of the Surang Bauri.

Begam Tank.—About two miles south of Bijapur is the old Begam tank, constructed by Muhammad Shah to supplement the water supply of the city. Afzal Khan had charge of the construction of the water towers and connecting pipes which brought in this water, and his name and date, 1651, occur in inscriptions on the towers near the Andu Masjid and the Asar Mahal.

The Ibrahimpur Mosque.—About a mile south of the city walls is the hamlet of Ibrahimpur, which is said to have been founded and colonized by Ibrahim I. in 1526, in which year he built the mosque which still stands near the village.

Ain-ul-Mulk's Tomb.—Standing about two miles away, to the east of Bijapur, is the tomb of Ain-ul-Mulk. It is a square massive looking building, surmounted by a very elegantly shaped dome. Within, upon the walls, is some very pretty stucco work in the shape of great pendants hanging down upon the face of each. This is the burial place of Ain-ul-Mulk, one of the officers of Ibrahim I., who rebelled against him and was killed near Bijapur in 1556. Beside the tomb is the mosque.

The Tomb of Jahan Begam.—Further away again, is the unfinished tomb of Jahan Begam. The plan of this building is exactly the same, both in size and design, as that of the great Gol Gumbaz. There are also the four corner towers as in the latter, but the four façades of the building were to be open, with three great arches in each face between the corner towers. The inner walls were intended to enclose the sepulchral chamber and carry the dome. It was thus not intended that this building should carry a monster dome like the Gol Gumbaz, the inner chamber, only, would have been covered by the dome, and the corridor, around, would have been covered in with a flat roof.

It is not quite certain whose tomb this is. It is generally supposed to cover the remains of Taj Jahan Begam, daughter of Sayyid Abdul Rehman, and wife of Sultan Muhammad. She must, then, have been his third wife, since two are buried in his own mausoleum beside his mistress Rhumba. It is possible it may be the tomb of the mother of Sultan Muhammad.

Kumatgi.—Kumatgi is now a small village, ten miles east of Bijapur, on the Hippargi road. It was, at one time, a place frequented by the nobles, and, perhaps, the court of Bijapur, as a pleasure resort; and, on one side of the lake, are the remains of many buildings, walls, and gateways. Chief among these, are several little pavilions with tanks and cisterns around about them. On the walls of one these, are some very remarkable and interesting frescoes, which must be over two hundred years old. Compared with western art their execution is not of a very high standard.

It has been said that the game of Polo is an Indian game. Here, in this little hunting chateau at Kumatgi, the statement is fully confirmed. Above an archway is a spirited representation of the game, where, not only the men, but the horses seem to enjoy the sport. Two horsemen have the ball between their sticks, which have the usual crook at the end, and each is trying to get possession of it by hooking it away from the other; two other horsemen, also armed with polo sticks, are standing off, watching and waiting for it to be released. Over an opposite arch is a hunting scene, where the hunters, mounted, are chasing tigers, leopards, and deer. Around the lower parts of these two arches is some very pretty bird ornament. There are also representations of persons, who, from their peculiar dress and light complexions, appear to be Europeans of note—possibly portraits of envoys or ambassadors who visited the Bijapur court. On another wall is the full length figure of a musician who plays upon a guitar whilst a queen and her maid sit listening. It is evident the musician, who, from his head-dress and flowing robes, might be a Persian, is trying to make an impression upon the ladies, for he holds his head on one side in a very lackadaisical manner as he plays. It reminds one strongly of a scene from "Lalla Rook," but for the absence of the crusty old chamberlain. But we have him here on another part of the walls, or a portrait that might well be his. Another, rather indistinct in parts, depicts a wrestling match that is going on before a seated and several standing figures.

On another wall are two seated figures clad in tiger skin garments, with tiger-face visors thrown up on the forehead. They are armed, and have their horses beside them. They appear to have met on the road, and are sitting under a tree, which has some most curiously shaped birds in its branches. Strapped on the arms of the two figures are guards, which are, no doubt, intended to take the place of shields in hand to hand contests.

The surface of the walls, and consequently the paintings, have suffered very great damage from having been scribbled over, scratched, and smoked. Kumatgi was evidently used by the nobles of Bijapur as a hunting centre, and the great artificial lake, upon the border of which several of these little chateaux stand, must have made it a favourite and pleasant resort. Its wild fowl attract the sportsman at the present day, and a trip to Kumatgi for a day's shooting is one of the pleasures the Bijapur folk still enjoy.

Here are extensive ruins of a small town or bazar, which appears to have been walled in ; and there is a long broad road, down each side of which is a fine row of stabling arcade for the horses of masters and followers. From this, a broad road led down, through a great gateway, along the margin of the lake and past the different pavilions.

Not the least of their enjoyments were the the cool refreshing fountains and cisterns. In fact, the elaborate waterworks, in and around these buildings, are their chief feature. Out in front of the painted pavilion, and rising out of a large square tank, is a two-storeyed building, through the masonry of which, pipes are carried up to scores of jets on both storeys. These all open outwards, and, when the water was turned on, and spouted forth from every conceivable point, falling splashing into the tank below, it must have been a very refreshing sight. The water was raised by manual labour to a cistern on the top of a high tower, and from this distributed, through pipes, to the various points below.

Not content with this grand display before the pavilion, they must needs have more of it within. From a large chunam-lined tank, on the roof, water was allowed to descend through a great perforated rose, in the centre of the ceiling, forming a magnificent shower bath, with a cistern below it to wallow in. What thorough enjoyment this must have been in the hot, dry weather! Surely those proud old warriors, who made the welkin ring with the clash of steel, knew, too, how to make the best of life in their idle moments!

ITINERARY.

MANY visitors to Bijapur allow themselves but one day in which to visit its buildings. It is needless to say that this is not, by any means, sufficient. For the convenience, however, of such visitors, routes Nos. 1 and 2 have been sketched out below, which include all the principal objects of interest. To avoid confusion, they should be followed in the order named, and, with the help of the map, at the end, this can easily be done. Only the places mentioned in black type should be visited, otherwise time will not suffice to go the round. To those who have the time, a week is not too long to spend at Bijapur,—in fact, Bijapur, and its surroundings, cannot be seen properly in less time. It might be crowded into four full days, but not comfortably.

1. If the visitor should arrive, as is generally the case, about midday, he should make preparations, as soon as possible, for an evening drive round the town; and, for this purpose, he should, with the help of the Travellers' Bungalow peon, or his own servants, arrange for a hired tonga from the town, or the railway station, to be ready at three o'clock in the afternoon at latest. It is best not to pay the tonga man for the journey from the Railway station at the time, but to order him to be back at the bungalow at three o'clock. Start for the great **Gol Gombaz,** which was passed

when coming from the station (see p. 20 for description). After examining this building, direct the driver to the Jami Masjid. Following the road due south, and crossing the road from the railway station to the citadel, 800 yards brings us to the next road, leading up to the Jami Masjid. The driver should be directed in the order of the names in black type. Just at the junction here, on the left hand side of the road, is the tomb of Pir Sayyid Haji Husain. Proceeding in a westerly direction, we pass, about three hundred yards from this, on the left, two ranges of solid heavy looking building known as Muhammad Shah's Granary. The length is divided into rooms for the storage of grain, the grain being filled in from holes in the roof, and drawn off from the doorways, which have grooves, top and bottom, for shutters. Another 450 yards brings us abreast of the **Jami Masjid**, (p. 29), the principal religious building in Bijapur.

After leaving this, and still proceeding west, 450 yards takes us past the Bari Kaman or arch, and the turning to Mustafa Khan's mosque, a litttle way up the road on the left. Beyond this great archway we pass a little mosque, standing out in the road. There is nothing remarkable about it, but the story of its origin shews what sanctity, in Muhammadan eyes, surrounds their mosques. It is stated that a certain man wished to build a mosque here, but the authorities objected to it as the site was in the main road. The man, under the pretence of performing a marriage ceremony, enclosed the space with *kanaths* or screens, and, under cover of these, erected the mosque.

The mosque, once built, could not be destroyed, even by the king, and it has so remained under the name of the Kanathi Masjid. Eight-hundred yards from the Jami Masjid finds us opposite the door of the **Mehtar Mahal**, (p. 32). Beyond this, on the left, is a range of arcade, terminating, at the corner, in the Pailu Mahal, now converted into a residence. At the back of this arcade, are the almost shapeless ruins of the old mint, with a garden which is still called the Taksal-ki-Bag or Mint Garden. At the end of the arcade we turn sharp round to the right, by a small corner mosque, and drive down to the **Asar Mahal** (p. 37). On our left are the high walls of the citadel, and on the right, near the Asar Mahal, we pass the Shah Ganj, one of the water towers erected by Afzal Khan (p. 95).

Returning up the same road, and, either passing through the citadel, (it is included in route No. 2, and need not take up attention now), or round the south side of it, we still drive west. On getting into the avenue, overshadowed with fine trees, a little way beyond the citadel, we pass on our left, in the fields, and just beyond the Forest Officer's bungalow, a great Adansonia tree of great girth. There were two, but the greater, of over 50 feet girth, has but lately fallen. Tradition says that it was under these the executions took place in the good old times. There are a few others in the suburbs. It is supposed they were introduced from Africa by some of the Abyssinians in the employ of the state. Just beyond this, on the left, are the "Two Sisters" or Jod Gumbaz, whose two similar domes have suggested the name, (p. 83). Still continuing along this same road, and entering the Mahmudshah Bazar, we soon come opposite the two high towers flanking the entrance to the **Taj Bauri**, (p. 43).

A hundred yards further on, at the end of this road, is a large doorway leading into an enclosure built around the old Makka gateway.

Turning north, at this point, and following the line of the old walls, we come to the foot of the bastion on which is the **Malik-i-Maidan** (p. 44). The ascent to it is under a tree which grows on the ramparts, a little way beyond a small police *chauki*, standing in the middle of the junction of two roads.

From the Malik-i-Maidan a road runs straight to the high tower, the **Haidar Burj** (p. 49). One hundred yards south of the Haidar Burj is the Dekhani Idgah (p. 88), and 250 yards east of this, just across the road leading to the Shahapur gate, is the Chota Asar Mahal (p. 87).

Returning by the road leading back to the Travellers' Bungalow, past the north side of the citadel, we pass the Bukhara Masjid, (p. 85), and come to the unfinished mausoleum of ALI (II.) ADIL SHAH (p. 52), which stands away off the road, to the left, behind some plantain gardens.

2. Very early next morning, the visitor might drive out to the **Ibrahim Rauza** (p. 53), outside the walls to the west of the town; and, after spending a little time at this group of buildings, return through the citadel, past the Janjiri Masjid (p. 82), the Sat Manjli, the

Gagan Mahal, and the Anand Mahal, to the Travellers' Bungalow. This will be about as much as is possible, if leaving by the morning train. If not, take up the buildings in the Arkilla or citadel. Starting from the north end of the citadel, and following the road running southward through the middle of it, we leave the **Adaulat Mahal**, and the **Arash Mahal**, the Civil Surgeon's residence, (p. 58), beyond it, on our left, and make for the great building, with its enormous arch,* before us on our right, beside the tennis ground. This is the **Gagan Mahal** (p. 60). On the left of the road, with its fine three-arched facade, is the **Anand Mahal** (p. 59), the residence of the Assistant Collector. In the same building, immediately behind it, is located the station library. The arch, connecting the two, is an experimental arch built by the Public Works Department. Turning to the right we find a little building at the south-east corner of the Gagan Mahal. This is an old building converted into a station church. South-west of this rise the five remaining storeys of the **Sat Manjli** (p. 61), with its adjacent buildings, the **Granary** (p. 66) and the **Chini Mahal** at its south end.

Sixty or seventy yards east of the Chini Mahal is the old mosque of **Malik Karim-ud-din** (p. 70). From this the visitor might go across to the **Makka Masjid** (p. 67) which is enclosed within the very high walls north-east from this. Near the walls is an old tower

---

* Its central arch is not, as has been supposed, the largest in Bijapur. The arch, under the viaduct, behind the Asar Mahal, is two feet greater in span.

called the Bichkanhalli tower, which has been supposed to be the old watch tower of the village of that name, and which existed here before the fort was built (p. 69). East of the Makka Masjid, and perched on the top of the ramparts, is the **Chinch Diddi Masjid** (p. 86). Across the moat, opposite to this, is the back of the Asar Mahal, and the ruin of several buildings immediately below it. Returning *via* the old mosque of Malik Karim-ud-din, and leaving the road exit, through the walls, on our left, we find ourselves in the old **Gateway of the Citadel** (p. 71) with its clusters of standing columns.

After an inspection of the gateway, the driver may be directed to the **Andu Masjid** (p. 73), or, if he does not know this, to the Police Superintendent Saheb's bungalow, which is on the same road. The Andu Masjid is known at a glance, standing upon the left hand side of the road, the mosque being on the second storey, with clusters of neat little minarets around its dome. Still proceeding along the same road, we pass the Police Superintendent's residence, which was once the ruins of the Chota Chini Mahal. At the end of this road, where it passes out through the walls, we halt, and proceed to inspect the largest gun in Bijapur, on the **Landa Qasab** (p. 75), the second bastion on the left or east of the road. A flight of narrow steps leads up to it. This completes the second tour.

3. Another trip may be taken to **Ali Shahid Pir's Mosque** (p. 78). Drive to the Bari Kaman, or great archway, between the

Jami Masjid and the Mehtar Mahal, and turn down the road opposite to it, running south. Proceed along this for about 250 yards to the first corner and stop, and, through a gap in the hedge on the right, the visitor will find a way into the field above. Across the field, west of him, about 150 yards off, he will see the object of his search.

Returning to the road, drive round to the Andu Masjid, already visited, and on to a point in front of the gateway of the residence of the Superintendent of Police. Here will be found a road, running west, past Ibrahim's old Jami Masjid, a hundred yards off the road to the right, to the **Tomb of Ali (I.) Adil Shah.** Due east of this, 400 yards, is the tomb of **Pir Shekh Hamid Qadir** (p. 63).

Direct the driver to the Nau Bag, passing round by the Andu Masjid. This is a favourite camping ground, and contains some fine large trees. Approaching it, the square walled enclosure of the **Begam Saheba's Rauza** is passed. Within is the burial place of Aurangzib's queen, who died at Bijapur of plague during the Emperor's stay here. A hundred yards to the south-east of this enclosure is **Kishwar Khan's Tomb,** with its unfinished brick dome (p. 6).

4. Drive to the **Janjiri Masjid** (p. 82) immediately west of the Sat Manjli, thence to the **Jod Gumbaz** or Khan Muhammad's Tomb (p. 83). Return and visit the **Bukhara Masjid** (p. 85), directing the driver to the Post Office; follow the cross road up past the east arcade of the Masjid to **Malik Sandal's Tomb**

close by (p. 86). Notice the neat little **Zamrud Masjid** (p. 84), on a raised platform by the roadside between these two buildings. It is the smallest mosque in Bijapur.

Passing up through the New Bazar, in a north-westerly direction from this, pass **Sikandar's Tomb**, a plain white-washed tomb in the open air, with a low wall round it, and continue in the same direction to the **Chota Asar** (p. 87). Now follow the road, to the **Shahapur Gate**, and a hundred yards, this side of it, is the **Chand Bauri** (p. 88).

5. This trip, if carried out in its entirety, will entail a little tramping; but if the visitor starts early, and does not mind a good walk, it will be very enjoyable, and the little trouble necessitated in preserving his bearings, and the slight risk of losing his way, will add to the enjoyment of the morning's outing.

Drive out very early to the **Amin Dargah** (p. 90) passing the **Jail** on the left. Dismounting, direct the driver to take the tonga away round to the fourth mile stone on the Torveh road or to the Muhammad Sarovar. A short distance north-west of the Amin Dargah is the masonry dam of the great Ramling Tank with its elaborate outlets. The tank does not now hold water, but the stream, which it once arrested, now runs peacefully down through the middle of it (p. 90). Southwest of this, about half a mile west of the village of Takki or Afzalpur, is the **Cenoatph, Mosque, and Ruins of the Palace of Afzal Khan** (p. 90). From this strike south to the **Tombs of Afzal Khan's Wives**

(p. 92), amongst a grove of trees; near this is the **Surang Bauri**, from which the great tunnel runs to Bijapur (p. 14). Half a mile south of this again is the Torveh road running east and west; but, just before reaching it, we cross the track of the great road of Muhammad Shah, leading from Torveh towards Bijapur. This is marked out by the parallel lines of mounds leading towards the Ibrahim Rauza. The distance, from the Amin Dargah to the road here, is about two and a half miles. The tonga should be waiting somewhere about here to take the visitor on to the **Sangat Mahal** (p. 93) and other ruins about Torveh, the remains of the city of Nauraspur. It would be better, if the visitor can afford the time, to make a separate trip to Torveh—a day's picnic—and wander about amongst its ruins.

6. The tombs at Ainapur, out on the east of Bijapur, will well repay a visit, (p. 95). Drive down the Kumatgi road, out by the opening through the walls between the Allahpur and Padshahpur gates, until abreast of the village of Ainapur, when a cart track will be found along which the tonga can proceed up to the village.

7. An exceedingly pleasant day may be spent out at **Kumatgi** (p. 96), ten miles east of Bijapur, with a well stocked tiffin basket, where, in the cold weather, duck shooting may be had. There are several little pavilions where one can put up during the heat of the day. Arrangements would have to be made, beforehand, for a tonga.

HISTORICAL OUTLINE.

On the death of Murad, Sultan of Turkey, in 1451, his eldest son Muhammad succeeded him. It was the custom in that country, on the death of a Sultan, for all his male children to be put to death excepting the heir. Yusaf, who was a younger brother of Muhammad, would thus have met with a violent death had not his mother, by stratagem, succeeded in averting it. Muhammad, too, is said to have wished to spare his brother's life, but his councillors so pressed upon him the advisability of carrying out the usual custom, that he at last asked them to allow him to consult his mother. The latter craved a day's grace to consider. It happened, at that time, that a certain merchant from Saver, named Khawjah Imad-ud-din Gargastani, was present in Constantinople trying to dispose of a consignment of merchandise and slaves. Yusaf's mother found among these slaves a boy who was remarkably like her son; so, handing over the latter to the merchant, with earnest entreaties for his safe keeping, she purchased the little stranger and secreted him in her own apartments. At midnight a great cry was raised that Yusaf had died, and, in the morning, the body of the little slave was carried away to burial, amid lamentations and all the honours befitting his supposed rank. Some say he was strangled, others that his foster-mother poisoned him.

The merchant was induced to leave the capital that night and return to his native town. He soon began to take a great interest in the young prince, and did his utmost to give him such an education as was due to his rank. In the year following Yusaf's departure from Constantinople, his mother sent his nurse, with others, to him, and, yearly after this, messengers were regularly dispatched by her to bring her news of her son's welfare. But, after a while, a whisper got abroad that a prince was in Saveh; and the governor, with a view to arresting him, entered into sham business relations with the merchant. Imad-ud-din, suspecting his intentions, and finding it unsafe to remain any longer in the town, left it, and went to live in a place called Kassim. On the death of the governor he thought of returning, but Yusaf, owing to a vision he had had, prevailed upon him to set out for Hindustan. In the vision, it is said, a man announcing himself as Khwaja Khizar, told him not to return to Saveh but to proceed to Hindustan, where all his wishes would be satisfied, and where he would, after many troubles and vexations, acquire a kingdom for himself. The purport of the vision he withheld from Imad-ud-din, but the latter, nevertheless, fell in with his wishes, and they both set out together in A.H. 864 (A.D. 1459-60.) They arrived at the port of Dabul where they resided for some time. Again did Yusaf have a vision, when Khwaja Khizar appeared to him a second time, with encouragement and good words. Imad-ud-din afterwords set out for Bidar, Yusaf accompanying him; and, owing to the influence of his adoptive father at the court of Sultan Muhammad Bahmani, Yusaf was taken on as one of the king's retainers.

Another account tells us that Yusaf was the son of Mahmud Beg, governor of Saveh; and that, when the latter was killed in battle, and his family and adherents dispersed, Yusaf Beg was brought up as a child at Ispahan, was taken thence to Shiraz, and finally came to India. In this account, the vision of his future prosperity is said to have occurred to him in the mosque at Lad, when a man appeared to him, and, placing some hot cakes in his hands, significantly added—"Your bread has been cooked in the Dekhan."

The former account is, perhaps, nearer the truth, for it receives confirmation in the fact that almost all the state buildings at Bijapur are, or have been, surmounted by the crescent, which is the emblem of the Sultans of Turkey.

Stories are related of his great skill in feats of arms, and how he overcame, in a wrestling match, before Sultan Muhammad and his nobles, the far-famed athlete of Dehli, who had come to Bidar with his pupils. His general appearance is much eulogised, and he is said to have been as generous and brave as he was handsome. He was, no doubt, a favourite at Bidar, and he rapidly rose in the king's favour. Promotion followed promotion quickly. It is not difficult to understand that, with such distinctions bestowed upon him, envy soon created many enemies for him, who were not long in finding an opportunity to damage his fair reputation. A disturbance broke out in the Telugu districts, and these men at once represented to the king that the very best man, whom he could send to quell it, was Yusaf. Yusaf was accordingly sent with a large force. But after he had been absent for some time, without any news having been received from him, Sultan Muhammad began to enquire the reason of his silence, and was told that he had taken possession of those districts, and had set himself up there as an independent prince. The true reason was that his enemies at court had intercepted his despatches, and withheld them from the king. He had, however, one true friend in Husain Aqa, who repudiated these charges, and begged that a certain Bada Aqa should be sent to bring news of him. On the departure of the latter, there was another long silence which Yusaf's enemies made the most of; and the king, getting uneasy, told Husain Aqa to go himself and fetch Yusaf back. Leaving Bada Aqa in charge of his troops and the district, Yusaf returned with Husain. On learning of his approach, Sultan Muhammad went out a short way to meet him, and, on hearing of how he had managed those troublous tribes he had been sent against, was so pleased at his success that he bestowed upon him the towns of Sanjan, Gudah, Ganchi, and Kastre, together with Bangalara, in *inam*. Bada Aqa was rewarded with the title of "Sajan Kali" and was instructed to reside in the Kanarese district.

Yusaf was, soon after, appointed governor of the Bijapur district with the title of "Adil

Khan." The last years of Sultan Muhammad saw the decline of the Bahmani kingdom; and, on his death, dissensions spread rapidly throughout the Bidar territories. Yusaf Adil Khan, collecting around him a strong force of Turks and Mughals, and, feeling himself pretty secure, began, by degrees, to sever his connection with the capital; and, finally, in A.D. 1489, he openly declared his independence by ordering the *khutba* to be read in the mosques in his own name.

Yusaf Adil Shah, 1489-1510.—He was not allowed to enjoy his new acquisitions long in peace, for Kasim Barid, minister at Bidar, collecting an army, marched against Bijapur and attacked him, being aided in this enterprise by Timraj of Vijayanagar. Yusaf, however, with great exertions, succeeded in repelling him, but the anxiety and worry attendant on it nearly cost him his life. He fell ill, and was confined to his apartments for two months, and, so bad was he, that at one time the news of his death spread through the town. On his recovery he distributed much money in alms, and gave 20,000 *huns* to Khwajah Abdulah Ardi to build a *minar* at the mosque at Saveh. He was again attacked, this time by Timraj. He set out to meet the enemy with 8,000 horsemen, but was at first driven back. Gathering around him 2,000 of of his best men he again led forward a fierce attack which the enemy was unable to withstand, and they, breaking up, fled in confusion. Yusaf obtained very great booty from this engagement, and returned to Bijapur much the richer for it.

Having, for a while, rid himself of his enemies, and having more time to devote to home matters, he bethought him to introduce into Bijapur the Shiah faith in which he had been brought up in Persia. The Muhammadans of the Dekhan were, as a body, followers of the Sunni persuasion, and, in consequence, resisted to the utmost these hated innovations. The opposition spread, and Mahmud of Bidar, with Ahmad Nizam Shah of Ahmednagar, and Kutub Shah of Golcondah, prepared for war in defence of their faith. Yusaf, unable to contend against this powerful combination, retreated into Khandesh and took shelter with his friend Imad-ul-mulk. The latter rated him soundly for his foolishness, and advised him to desist from trying to force the new faith upon his unwilling subjects, and, at the same time, he wrote to Mahmud telling him that Yusaf had given up the idea, and asked him to withdraw his forces from Bijapur. This was done, and Yusaf returned to his capital in peace. Nevertheless, he appears, subsequently, to have made another attempt to introduce the rival faith.

Toward the end of his reign news was received that the Portuguese had taken possession of Goa. Yusaf set out for its recovery, and, in five days, reached the fort and retook it. In the twenty-second year of his reign Yusaf died. Being conscious of the approach of death he summoned his son Ismail, and, declaring him his heir, had him crowned in his presence. He then gave over the management of the state, Ismail being a minor, to his minister Kamal Khan Dekhani, and desired him to bury him near the tomb of Shah Chanda Husaini in Gogi, a village he had received in *inam* from the Bidar king. His death is variously placed at A.H. 913, 916, and 925; but A.H. 916, that given by Ferishta, is generally taken as correct, *i.e.* A.D. 1510. Yusaf had but one son, Ismail, and three daughters. The latter were Khadijah Sultana, married to Ala-ud-din Bada Ruwala, son of Imad-ul-mulk of Berar, Mariam or Karima Sultana, married to Sultan Burhan Nizam Shah of Ahmednagar, and Bibi Sati, who was married to Ahmad Shah, son of Sultan Mahmud Bahmani of Bidar.

The citadel or "Ark" is said to have been built by Yusaf in 918 (A.D. 1512-13). This date is evidently given on the assumption that he lived beyond 1510, perhaps to A.H. 925, *i.e.*, A.D. 1519-20. An inscription on the citadel walls, engraved on a long white slab, between the Asar Mahal and the south gateway to the citadel, gives the date A.H. 920, *i.e.*, A.D. 1514-15, of the building of some part of the same; but the language is barbarous and verbose and its purport is not very clear. Other inscriptions in and about the citadel gate are of the time of Ibrahim I. The Dekhani Idgah, near the Upri Burj, is also ascribed to Yusaf, although an inscription on it says that "this place of prayer was built by Malik the Khajah of the period, Ghaflat, in the year 945" during the reign of Ibrahim. A very small old mosque, usually known as Yusaf's old Jami Masjid, situated a little way east of the Mehtar Mahal, and off the road, has an inscription which informs us that—"This mosque was built during the period of Sultan Mahmud Shah, son of Muhammad Bahmani. Its cost was defrayed by Asen Beg Nayib Ghibet Adil Khani, A.H. 918," (A.D. 1512-13). In this the reign of the Adil Shahis is quite ignored. If Yusaf died in 1510 then this must have been built during the minority of Ismail, when the traitor Kamal Khan was intriguing with Kasim Barid, and therefore, at a time when the Bahmani court had more or less influence, through its minister, over Bijapur affairs. Yusaf is said, also, to have erected a *minar* at Gulburgah.

Bijapur does not seem to have been a place of much importance before the time of Yusaf. The earliest authentic records we have of the place are contained in the old Kanarese inscriptions on the tablet and columns at the entrance to the citadel. These columns and other fragments are remains of several Hindu temples which once existed on or near this spot. The Muhammadans probably found these shrines partly in ruins, and set about to use the materials to construct their gateways, guardrooms, and mosques. It is what they did in Gujarat and other parts of the country. In the old mosque, a few hundred yards north of this gateway, which is entirely made up of old Hindu temple materials, the porch is really part of a temple *in situ*,—it is the hall or *mandapa* undisturbed. The shrine, which joined it on the west, was, of course, pulled down.

The principal inscription is a well inscribed slab which had been built in, low down, on the left side of the inner gate of the citadel. It is of the time of the Western Chalukya king Bhuvanaikamalla or Somesvara II., and is dated in *Saka* 996 (A. D. 1074-5).* From this inscription it is known that Bijapur was then included in the district known as the Taddevadi Thousand (Tuddehwarree of the maps, on the south bank of the Bhima, 36 miles north of Bijapur), and which, at that time, was governed by the king's *dandanayaka* Nakimayya. It records the building of the temple of the god Sri-Svayambhu-Siddhesvara at the capital of Vijayapura, and a grant of 300 *mattars* of land in the lands of Bijjanhalli, which was included in the Konnuvuri Twelve. Mr. Fleet believes these places to be Kunoor and the Busnal of the maps, seventeen and eighteen miles respectively from Bijapur. The last few lines of this inscription are of a later date, and were added in the time of Vikramaditya VI. Bijapur was thus a Western Chalukyan possession in the 11th century, and, from inscriptions of subsequent date on some of the pillars in the gateway, we find that it must have passed into the hands of the Yadavas, in whose possession it was in the latter half of the 12th and beginning of the 13th centuries. During the invasion of Malik Kafur, Ala-ud-din's general, about 1310, the Muhammadans occupied Bijapur, and an inscription on a pilaster in the converted temple, just mentioned, tells us, Malik Karim-ud-din erected the upper part of the mosque in S. 1242 (A.D. 1320). Karim-ud-din was the son

* Indian Antiquary, Vol. X., p. 126.

of Malik Kafur, and appears to have resided here as governor.

From the Chalukya inscription it is plain that the name of the place was originally Vijayapura, or "city of victory," probably so called on account of some victory having at one time been obtained here, and this name has remained to it, with brief intermissions, to the present day under the Muhammadan form of Bijapur. In the vernacular it is written Vijapur. The intermissions were, as local historians tell us, when Ibrahim II., in 1603, gave it the name of Badyapur, and when Sultan Muhammad called it Muhammadpur.*

Ismail Adil Shah, 1510-1534.—Ismail is said to have been about twelve or thirteen years old when he succeeded his father. As already mentioned, Kamal Khan was appointed regent, and, being a Sunni, he re-established that faith in Bijapur. Kamal Khan, in his new and responsible position, was not long in arrogating to himself powers which belonged to the king alone; and soon he began to aspire to that high position. He began by distributing lucrative appointments to his particular friends. In consultation with Amir Barid he laid a plot to dethrone Ismail, and so far carried out his evil designs that he imprisoned the young king in the Khatonan Mahal. He set out against Sholapur and took that fort after a three months siege. On

* In a Devanagari inscription on a wall near the Ibrahim Rauza, written in the time of Sultan Muhammad, Bijapur is called Vidyapura, or "city of wisdom." But this is probably due to the pedantry of the pandit who composed the inscription.

his return to Bijapur Kamal Khan was anxious to have himself proclaimed king without further delay, and, for this purpose, he summoned the astrologer to fix upon an auspicious day. They told him that the first fifteen days would be unlucky and were fraught with evil for him, and advised him to be on his watch during that interval against some undefined calamity. To avoid this he shut himself up in his own apartments after giving over charge of state affairs to his son Saftdar Khan, intending to remain in seclusion until the time was past. But inexorable fate followed him into his hiding place. Ismail's mother, Punji Khatun, on learning of the extent of Kamal Khan's evil designs, set to to devise means to circumvent them ; and, to this end, she and her relative Dilshad Aga arranged a little plot with a devoted slave named Kaka. Khatun then induced one of Kamal Khan's female servants to go and inform her master that Kaka was desirous of going on a pilgrimage to Makka, but that he wished to take formal leave from the minister before starting. He was admitted to his presence, and, as Kaka bent forward to receive the betel leaf at the hand of Kamal Khan, he rapidly withdrew a dagger from his waist band and plunged it into the traitor's bowels, killing him on the spot. Kaka was immediately cut down by the guards, who hurried in upon hearing the groans of their dying master. Kamal Khan's wife rushed in from the female apartments, and, with great presence of mind, and unusual coolness, repressed her emotions, checked Saftdar Khan, who, coming in then, was about to give the alarm, and ordered him to lose no time in issuing orders to the troops in Kamal Khan's name to arrest Ismail and his mother.

The long absence of Kaka on his mission caused great uneasiness to Punji Khatun, who began to fear that the plot had failed, and she anticipated the worst. She cheered Ismail and told him to be bold and brave. She then exhorted the men of the palace to be firm and loyal to their king in the approaching crisis, and they would, for their devotion, be well rewarded in this world and the next. Some craven hearts, however, fearing the wrath of Kamal Khan, went over to his side and joined Saftdar Khan. The latter, after rapidly collecting a strong force, advanced on the king's palace and forced the first and second gates. During this time the palace was stoutly defended, arrows flew thick and fast on the assailants, and Punji Khatun herself, clad in male attire, and armed with shield and sword, moved about amongst her men and urged them on to their utmost. In this defence she was nobly assisted by the king's adherents from other parts of the city, who got into the palace by means of ropes thrown over the walls. The opposite party was encouraged in its attack by the presence of Kamal Khan's body propped up at a window, opposite the palace, as if still alive but badly wounded. The attacking party are said to have been armed with muskets, and they would, no doubt, have prevailed in the end had not an event happened which changed the fortunes of the day. In the hottest part of the struggle, after Saftdar Khan had got access to the courtyard of the palace, which was being obstinately defended from the terrace above, he was sorely wounded in the hand by an arrow, and moved off to one side, under the walls, to sit down. The opportunity was at once seized upon by the defenders, who rolled over an immense stone upon him, which crushed him as he sat there. Some say Ismail himself rolled the stone over, but it is more likely that it was done by others, for the boy Ismail would hardly have been allowed to expose himself on the walls. Saftdar Khan's death had an immediate effect upon his followers, who at once lost heart and fled. They were pursued by the palace troops, and the latter were much amazed to find, when they entered his house, that Kamal Khan was already dead. As soon as he was again in possession of his rights, Ismail rewarded those who so fearlessly stood by him, and to Khusro Aqa, one of his most faithful attendants, he gave the title of Asad Khan with the fort of Belgaum in *jaghir*. He dismissed all the Dekhanis and Negroes from the state service, and began to employ Mughals. Thus, with the aid of the latter, who were good archers and spearmen, he so strengthened his position that he followed up his father's efforts to establish the Shiah faith, and thereupon ordered it to be the state creed.

As soon as Ismail had pretty well consolidated his little kingdom, he began to look around him and prepare for further conquests. He first raided the districts of Kasim Barid, which compelled the latter to seek the assistance of Burhan Nizam Shah of Ahmednagar, Kutub Shah, and Imad-ul-Mulk. The combined forces invaded the Bijapur district, and plundered it up to the very gates of the capital itself. Here Ismail fell upon them with 12,000 Mughal horse and utterly routed them, taking Mahmud and his son Ahmad Shah prisoners. These he conducted, with great respect and honour, into the city, and had their wounds attended to. He then proposed that the marriage of Bibi Sati, his sister, with Ahmad Shah should take place. This was carried out at Gulburgah, and, immediately after, he dismissed Mahmud and party, who were well pleased with his generous treatment, and sent them back to Bidar with an escort of honour of 5,000 horse.

Owing to the unbearable insolence of Timraj of Vijayanagar, Asad Khan, who had attained to the high position of commander-in-chief, endeavoured to bring about a coalition between his master and Nizam Shah for the purpose of punishing this haughty rival, and, to this end, he sent an experienced official, named Kayyid Ahmad Harvi, with presents to Ahmednagar. Ismail's sister, Mariam Sultana, was given in marriage to Nizam Shah, and the fort of Sholapur was promised as part of the dowry. But Ismail subsequently refused to carry out the latter part of his promise, upon which Burhan Nizam Shah determined to take it by force, and applied to Imad-ul-Mulk for assistance. Ismail went out to meet him with 12,000 men, and a battle ensued, in which Nizam Shah's troops broke up and fled, and were pursued up to the gates of the fort of Parandah. In this action Ismail captured forty elephants, ten of which he presented to Asad Khan, and some he gave to other nobles. Again did Nizam Shah and Amir Barid attack him but were defeated, and, this time, twenty elephants fell to the lot of the latter. He kept one of these, named "Allah Baksh," for his own use, and gave the rest to Asad Khan. After this, Asad Khan tried his best to bring about a friendly feeling between Ismail and Ala-ud-din Imad-ul-Mulk, and Khadijah, Ismail's sister, was betrothed to the Berar potentate.

For offence given by Amir Barid, Ismail with 10,000 horse, invaded the Bidar territory. He pushed forward his forces until he arrived at the capital, and at once proceeded to lay siege to the fort. He detailed half of his force, under Asad Khan, to intercept Kutub Shah who had come to the assistance of Amir Barid. Asad Khan soon repulsed the forces of Kutub Shah and immediately returned and joined his division with the king's in the general siege. Amir Barid, hard pressed, sought the mediation of Imad-ul-Mulk, who had, with his army, joined Ismail; but the latter warned Imad-ul-Mulk not to interfere in this matter as he was determined to take revenge ere he quitted his position. Imad-ul-Mulk, who was rather inclined to take the part of Amir Barid, on receiving this message, abstained from any interference, but Barid, much distressed, came to his tent and besought him to intercede for him. Imad-ul-Mulk explained to him that peace was impossible until he surrendered the fort.

Barid finding his entreaties of no avail, gave himself up to drink and debauchery in his own encampment. Asad Khan Lari, on getting news of this, went at night to his camp, together with a handful of trusty followers, and, entering his tent, took up the bedstead on which the drunken Barid lay. Two half inebriated servants, who were awake in the tent, were dispatched before any alarm could be raised by them. When clear of the camp, the bearers set up the *kalmeshadal*, or funeral dirge, and, as they got nearer their own quarters, began to cry it more loudly. Owing to the jolting, and the noise, and his rapid passage through the fresh night air, Amir Barid partly recovered his senses and began to think the ghosts were carrying him off, and, jumping up, he shouted "lahol."* "I am no ghost to be scared by your, 'lahol'" cried Asad Khan. Hearing his voice, Amir Barid at once realised his position, and commenced most humbly to ask pardon and crave for life. Asad Khan promised to do all he could for him, and, carrying him off to Ismail, related the whole story of his capture.

The next morning Amir Barid was brought up before the king, but the latter, to humble him to the utmost, allowed him to stand, for a long time, waiting in the hot sun bare-foot and bare-headed. When he was brought into his presence, Ismail ordered his immediate execution. The unfortunate prisoner craved hard for his life, promising the cession of the

---

* A charmed exclamation which is supposed to drive ghosts and devils away.

forts of Umnabad and Bidar with their treasure, and Asad Khan also pleaded that his life might be spared. On these conditions it was granted, and Amir Barid sent word to his sons in the fort to give it up ; but they at first refused, thinking that, by delaying, they might eventually get better terms. But Ismail, not to be trifled with, ordered an elephant to be got ready which was to drag Barid, chained to its foot, to the gate of the fort, so that he might be trampled to death before the eyes of his sons. This had the desired effect, and they gave up the fort without further delay. Ismail entered in great state, and, seating himself on the Bahmani *masnad*, distributed the treasure found there. At the instance of Imad-ul-Mulk, Amir Barid was pardoned and provided for. The fort of Bidar was given in charge of Mustafa Khan Shirazi.

After this Ismail marched against Madgal and Raichor and possessed himself of both these forts. Amir Barid, by his cringing and flattery, soon worked round the heart of Ismail, and the latter promised to give him Bidar again. This he fulfilled later on, reserving to himself Kalyana and Khandar. But Kasim Barid was no sooner in possession of his own again than he began to shew the old spirit, and joined with Burhan Nizam Shah in a war against Bijapur. They took the field with 25,000 horse and a battery of artillery, but Ismail and Asad Khan, with a force of 2,000 horse, soon obliged this great force to retreat. Khurshed Khan, the eldest son of Nizam Shah, was killed in the action that was fought, and Nizam

Shah's elephants, battery, and other material of war, fell into the hands of Ismail. Subsequently these two kings met, and agreed that Ismail should possess himself of the country of Kutub Shah, while Nizam Shah should take that of Imad-ul-Mulk, and that they should thenceforth live in peace.

After enjoying a time of peace and freedom from foreign wars, Ismail once again roused himself to action and set out against Golcondah. During the siege of this place he fell sick, and, his case becoming hopeless, he rapidly sank and died at Sagar in A.H. 941 (A.D. 1534.) His body was sent to Gogi and laid beside his father's.

He is said to have laid the foundation of Chandapur * in A.H. 926 (A.D. 1520,) and to have built the Champa Mahal † in A.D. 927 (A.D. 1521.) A local historian thus sums up his character: "He was just, patient, and liberal; extremely generous, frequently pardoning state criminals, and averse to listening to slander. He never used passionate language, and possessed great wit, to which he added a sound and accurate judgement. He was an adept in the arts of painting, varnishing, making arrows, and embroidering saddle cloths; and in music and poetry excelled most of his age. He supported literary men and scholars munificently at his court; and had a great fund of humour, which he displayed at his private parties and in familiar

---

* A village a few miles south of Bijapur.

† No vestige of this palace now remains.

intercourse with his courtiers."* He was much loved by his soldiers and was a brave warrior himself.

Mallu Adil Shah, 1534.—It was Ismail's dying wish that the rightful heir, Mallu, his eldest son, should succeed him, and this he desired Asad Khan to see to. This was accordingly carried out, but Mallu so disgusted every one by his evil ways and bad character that it was no difficult task to those who heartily wished it, among whom were his grandmother, Punji Khatun, and Asad Khan, to depose him. After a short reign of seven months he was accordingly set aside and blinded, and his younger brother Ibrahim was hailed king in his stead.

Ibrahim (I.) Adil Shah, 1534—1557.—It was a great relief to all when Ibrahim was seated upon the throne in the place of the libertine Mallu, and his subjects soon learned to have confidence in him. He was a brave man and a good soldier, and he was more or less engaged in war throughout his reign. It is said he was ever on the alert, and hardly slept at night, being always in a state of unrest, and in perpetual anticipation of sudden inroads by his enemies. It is told of Tahmasp, king of Persia, that he used to say that two kings, Afrasiab Turk and Ibrahim Adil Shah, had no other rivals in deeds of bravery and heroism.

He inaugurated his reign by introducing drastic measures of reform in the civil administration of the state. He restored the Sunni

---

**Students' Manual of the History of India.* Meadows Taylor. p. 206

faith, and, as a consequence, dismissed the majority of those from office who had been brought in by his ancestors to swell the number of the Shiahs. He re-employed Dekhanis and Abyssinians in place of the discharged Persians and others; and the Hindu element in the public offices was considerably increased. Persian was exchanged for Marathi as the official language.

Bhoj Tarmal, the rightful sovereign of Vijayanagar, determined to make another attempt to oust Ramraj, the usurper, and called upon Ibrahim to assist him in this undertaking. But when the latter had arrived on the scene with a great army, Ramraj wrote a most humble and abject apology to Bhoj Tarmal, confessing his crime, and saying he would rather throw himself upon his mercy than that the Muhammadans should be allowed to overrun the land. He graphically described to him the horrors and insults that would result from this; that the Muhammadans would destroy the country, break down their shrines, and carry off their wives and daughters. Bhoj Tarmal, deceived by his assumed humility, sent forty or more lacs of *huns* to Ibrahim to pay the expenses of his expedition, and besought him to return. Ibrahim, quite as well pleased with ready cash as with a bloody engagement, returned to Bijapur; but he was no sooner gone than Ramraj returned to Vijayanagar, murdered the too confiding Bhoj Tarmal, and assumed the full powers of royalty. Ibrahim, on his return home, is said to have laid out part of the money thus obtained in strengthening and completing the citadel fortifications, and this is confirmed by the inscriptions on the walls. One, on the inside of the south gate, dated in A. H. 945 (A. D. 1538), in the third or fourth year of his reign, records the building of the "Elahi Burj" or Divine Bastion. He is accredited with having built the double lines of walls with their ditches. Perhaps, he improved and strengthened, with more solid masonry, the walls already built by Yusaf and Ismail.

On hearing of the death of Bhoj Tarmal, and perhaps thinking that he had as much right to some of the Vijayanagar possessions as Ramraj, Ibrahim despatched Asad Khan with considerable forces to take the fort of Adoni. Ramraj sent his brother Venkatadari with an army to oppose Asad Khan. Asad Khan at first had to retreat, but, immediately rallying, made an onslaught upon Venkatadari, when the Vijayanagar troops fled leaving everything on the field, even to their leader's children, who were made captive. These were eventually restored to Venkatadari. Ibrahim was so pleased with this victory that he promoted Asad Khan, gave him rich presents and his daughter in marriage, declaring that if she had a son by him that son should be his heir. About this time one of the king's nobles, Ain-ul-Mulk Kanani, rebelled and took possession of several districts adjoining his *jaghir*, but Ibrahim promptly confronted him and obliged him to flee to the Court of Nizam Shah where he expected to find favour. Nizam Shah, not wishing at that time to allow anything to bring about a quarrel between himself and Ibrahim, had Ain-ul-Mulk put to death.

The old story, that when a man rose to importance in the state, and in favour with the king, there immediately grew up around him a prolific crop of envious backbiters, who were ever ready to slander him, and bring his good repute into question, became true of Asad Khan. His enemies now asserted that he was in league with Nizam Shah and was about to give up the fort of Belgaum, his own *jaghir*, to him. Ibrahim, thrown off his guard, and believing these stories, remonstrated with Asad Khan and ordered his arrest. This ill-feeling between the king and his military leader gave Nizam Shah a good opportunity to attack Bijapur, and so, in conjunction with Khwajah Jahan Dekhani, and Ali Barid, he made inroads into the Bijapur territories. He took the fort of Sholapur and made for Belgaum, believing that, as their relations were so strained, Asad Khan would break with the king and make over the fort to him. Asad Khan, taking care not to undeceive Nizam Shah for the present, secretly sent a message to Imad-ul-Mulk telling him of the straits Ibrahim had got into, and asked hisassistance. Imad-ul-Mulk straightway marched to Gulburgah, where Ibrahim was encamped, and explained to him the whole business. The king was very much vexed with himself for harbouring these suspicions about Asad Khan and immediately sent for him. Now that the two were reconciled and worked together, they, with the assistance of Imad-ul-Mulk, soon drove Nizam Shah out of the Bijapur dominions, invaded his own, and followed him up to Bid, taking back Sholapur and all other lost possessions, while Nizam Shah retreated to Daulatabad for safety.

The chief bone of contention between the Ahmednagar and Bijapur courts was the possession of this fort of Sholapur. A strong position, situated on the borders of the two kingdoms, it was a much desired possession by either as a fortified outpost. The loss of this was thus a severe blow to Nizam Shah, and he soon set about to retake it. To this end he induced Ramraj to break off friendly relations with Bijapur, and, calling upon Jamshed Kutub-ul-Mulk to join him, he re-opened hostilities by laying siege to that fort. Thus beset by Nizam Shah at Sholapur, Jamshed marching upon Bijapur from the north-east, and Kamraj committing devastations in the south-east, Ibrahim was rather hard pressed, and the outlook appeared gloomy enough. In this crisis heconsulted Asad Khan, who advised him to try and appease two of confederates and thus be at liberty to punish the third. This was done by the cession of Sholapur to Nizam Shah, who, thus satisfied, retired. Ramraj was conciliated in a similar manner. Asad Khan Lari now advanced against Kutub Shah and forced him back into the Telugu districts, following him up to Golconda. Here the latter made a determined stand, and a conflict ensued, in which Asad Khan and Kutub Shah met and fought with each other hand to hand, when Kutub Shah received such a cut from the sword of Asad Khan that he was disfigured for life. In the end the Bijapur troops prevailed, and Asad Khan returned to Bijapur in triumph.

The old enmity between Ahmednagar and Bijapur again broke out, and Nizam Shah once more marched against the city. He was opposed on the banks of the Bhima. The passages were blocked, but Ibrahim eventually managed to cross, and one of the fiercest encounters of his reign took place here. Again and again did he renew the attack, and, in the final assault, he drove home the charge so well that the Ahmednagar troops, having exhausted their ammunition, fled in confusion. Great loot fell into the hands of the victors. They took 135 elephants and 120 guns, together with much of the royal insignia that was left upon the field.

Ibrahim, although a very brave man, who fought personally hand to hand in most of his engagements, had a very fiery temper and was exceedingly harsh, meting out the most severe punishment for the most trifling offence. This undue severity after a time became so unbearable that a plot was formed to dethrone him and to place Abdulah on the throne. But before it could be put into execution, the news leaked out, and Ibrahim, coming to hear of it, immediately executed one hundred and ten nobles, both Hindu and Musalman, whom he suspected of being concerned in it. Prince Abdulah fled and sought protection with the Christians of Goa. Ibrahim also suspected Asad Khan Lari, his old and trusted general, who had retired to his *jaghir* at Belgaum, and imprisoned all his servants and followers that he found in the capital. By Asad Khan's earnest entreaties for their liberation, and his protestations against the charge of treason, Ibrahim grew ashamed of his conduct towards him, and determined to go and visit him personally, and make amends for the ill-treatment of his servants. As he approached Belgaum he heard of Asad Khan's death. He mourned his loss very much, and distributed goods and jewels among his sons. Asad Khan is said to have been over one hundred years old, and to have served the state of Bijapur forty or fifty years. He died in A.H. 956 (A. D. 1549) and is buried in the tomb he built for himself near the fort of Belgaum. One writer puts his death in A. H. 965 (A. D. 1557), the year of Ibrahim's death. It would seem that some clerical error had crept in in one or the other, and the 5 and the 6 had changed places. Asad Khan was, no doubt, one of the greatest men in Bijapur story, and since his death, for some reason or other, he is still remembered and treated as a *wali* or saint, religious discourses being occasionally delivered at his tomb.

Although Ibrahim possessed such a vindictive nature, yet he treated his soldiers well, and was courteous and urbane to learned men. He had four sons and two daughters; and, although their order of birth is not very clear, it seems evident that Ismail was older than Ali. The former was dull and stupid while the latter was bright and active, and the king, not liking the heir to be shown off to such disadvantage by contrast with his younger brother, had the latter confined to the fort of Miraj for nine years. The other sons were Ahmad and Tahmasp. His daughters were Hidayat Sultana, who was married to Murtaza Nizam Shah of Ahmednagar, and Tani Bibi, who afterwards became the bride of Ali Barid. Ibrahim appears to have contracted several diseases, and to have suffered much from them for two years. His doctors could not cure him, and were so severely punished for their failures that eventually none would go near him, and he was allowed to drag out the last few months of his misery without their aid. He died in A.H. 965 (A.D. 1557), and his body was carried to Gogi, with becoming pomp and ceremony, and buried beside his father's tomb. He reigned 23 years.

He colonised Ibrahimpur in A.H. 932 (A.D. 1526), and built the mosque in that suburb in the same year. He also built the Sola Thami Mahal in A.H. 935 (A.D. 1528), strengthened the fortifications of the citadel, and erected the Ghalib (victorious) Masjid, which was adorned with 1303 niches for lamps. Another building of his was the old Jami Masjid, near the tomb of Hazrat Jaffar Sakkaf, built in A.H. 958 (A. D. 1551), which still exists.

Ali (I.) Adil Shah, 1557—1580.—Ali's release from the fort of Miraj, or Murtazabad as it was also called, and his accession to the throne was hailed with satisfaction by almost all. It is said that endeavours were made by his father to set him aside in favour of Tahmasp, grandson of Asad Khan Lari, but that these were thwarted by his nobles, whose preference lay with Ali. A very strong reason for

Ibrahim's aversion to Ali was that the latter, despite his father's many threats and commands, was a firm adherent of the Shiah faith, and this was fostered by the companionship of Fateh Ulla Shirazi, his guardian. Ali answered his father's arguments by telling him that if he thought proper to depart from his father's faith, it was quite as admissable for him, Ali, to do the same. So, on ascending the throne, he again introduced the Shiah faith, and invited men of that persuasion, from Persia and elsewhere, to Bijapur in order to strengthen his party. The Sunnis were on the point of proclaiming a *jehad*, and disorder was imminent, but he at length won over the populace by his justice, liberality, and kindly manner. He did not spare his treasury, but lavished his wealth freely.

Ali Adil Shah commenced his reign by cultivating the friendship of Ramraj, and he paid a visit of condolence to him at Vijayanagar on hearing of the death of his son. Great festivities went on during his stay there, presents were freely exchanged, and, on his return to his capital, a deputation of nobles waited on him from Ramraj to pay their respects. Husain, who had succeeded Burhan Nizam Shah, had failed to send the customary letter of congratulation to Ali Adil Shah on his ascending the *masnad*. For this and other reasons, Ali Adil Shah determined to carry war and devastation into his territories; and in this he was willingly aided by Ramraj. Nizam Shah retreated to Daulatabad, and was followed up by the united forces, Ramraj's men pillaging and laying waste the country in all directions. They were not content with this, but gave offence to Ali Adil Shah by always seizing upon the best positions for their camps, and turning the Bijapur troops out of the good camping grounds they had chosen. For the present Ali Adil Shah overlooked these things but did not forget them. Eventually peace was concluded on Nizam Shah giving up Kalyan, and the Bijapur and Vijayanagar troops returned home.

Nizam Shah only wanted time to gather further troops and strengthen himself anew for another struggle with Ali Adil Shah ; and, by giving his daughter Jamal Bibi in marriage to Kutub Shah, he secured the latter's assistance. Ali Adil Shah again applied to Ramraj for aid, which the latter was only too ready to give for the sake of the prospect of plundering the country. The opposing forces met, and the action resulted in the defeat and flight of Nizam Shah. He even left upon the field the green flags which were the gift of the kings of Gujarat, and of which the Nizams of Ahmednagar were proud. Ali, possessing himself of these, put aside his own yellow banners, and in triumph displayed these new trophies. Before returning to Bijapur he rebuilt the fort of Naldrug. On their way home, after parting from Ali Shah, the Vijayanagar troops played havoc with the towns and country in their way, desolating mosques and tombs, and doing everything in their power to pay off old scores by insulting the Muhammadan religion.

Ali Adil Shah had now got thoroughly disgusted with the arrogance and overbearing pride of this *kafir* king, and, as both Nizam Shah and Kutub Shah had good cause, too, to wish him and his kingdom exterminated, it was no difficult task to induce these kings to join him in a great war against this infidel. To seal the compact with Nizam Shah, Ali Adil Shah gave his sister Hidayat Sultana in marriage to prince Murtaza, son of Nizam Shah, and, in return, the latter gave his daughter, the famous Chand Bibi, to Ali Adil Shah together with the fort of Sholapur. Ali Barid of Bidar also joined the confederacy; and the whole body marched in the direction of Vijayanagar in December, 1564. At the Krishna, south of Talikot, they found Ramraj, with immense forces, encamped on the other side and holding the fords of the river. Finding their means of progress stopped, the Muhammadans had recourse to a ruse. They sent on men up the river, some little distance, to gather boats and other means of crossing, and they followed leisurely themselves. The enemy, deceived by this move, crowded up the river to defend the upper fords, leaving the lower ones almost undefended. This was what the Muhammadans expected; and doubling back sharp during the night, they crossed at the fords before the Vijayanagar troops awoke to a sense of their negligence and danger. The latter fell back, and now took place one of the greatest of Indian battles, memorable for having decided the fate of the great kingdom of Vijayanagar. The two armies rapidly drew up in battle array some miles south of the river. The Muhammadan front was formed up with Ali Adil

Shah on the right, Kutub Shah and Ali Barid on the left, and Nizam Shah, with his artillery, in the centre. Ramraj's pride knew no bounds, and it eventually cost him his life; for, spurning the entreaties of his attendants to be mounted, he said his enemies were not worth it, and he remained seated in his palankin. When he found the Muhammadans pressing him heavily, he had his silken tent pitched and his treasure brought and placed about him, and he promised rich rewards to his troops when they should make the Muhammadans fly. The display of this promised treasure so incited his men that the Muhammadans were for a time driven back, but Nizam Shah, hastily summoning to his aid Kutub and Barid, soon regained his lost ground. In fact the Muhammadans, at this crisis, were so hard pressed that Nizam Shah, fearing it was going ill with them, determined to put himself in the thickest of the fight and become a *shahadat* * ; and at the same time he gave swords to the eunuchs of his harem with instructions to put his wives to death if they saw him fall.

Ali Adil Shah, with his artillery, attacked Talmraj, the elder brother of Ramraj, and forced him back into the main body under Ramraj. This caused the utmost confusion and disorder in his ranks, and Ramraj soon realised the ugly fact that he was completely surrounded by the Muhammadans. Nizam Shah, finding Ali Adil Shah's position on his right vacant, began

* One killed in war in defence of the faith, and therefore a martyr, receiving a martyr's reward.

to be very anxious as he did not know of the latter's successful flanking movement, and calling up Rumi Khan, the officer in charge of his artillery, ordered his guns into action. The sudden discharge of the battery had an immediate effect; the enemy's elephants took fright, and there was soon a general stampede of men, horses, and elephants in dire confusion. Each man looked to his own safety; officers forsook their troops, and troops deserted their officers; even the personal attendants of the great Ramraj fled from the field terror-stricken, and left him to the tender mercies of of his enemies. Rumi Khan, following up, stumbled upon him badly wounded, with none save his faithful relative Dilpatrao by him. Rumi Khan hurried off with his captive to Nizam Shah, and the latter was at first rather disposed to be lenient with him; but being reproached by Kasim Beg Tabrezi, a relative, with shewing favour to a *kafir*, he at once ordered his head to be struck off. When the Hindus saw their leader's head hoisted up aloft upon a spear they knew all hope was gone, and those few, who were still making any stand, fled from the field. The Muhammadans followed them up for miles, and the country between the field of battle and Anagundi was strewn with the dead and dying. It is said that it took the clerks and others twelve days to number the slain and wounded. It is estimated that, without exaggeration, there must have been at least 150,000 troops engaged in this battle.

For twenty days the combined forces halted to allow of their wounded being attended to, and then marched into Vijayanagar where they remained for some time. The greater part of the city was destroyed, and Vijayanagar was henceforth blotted out from the roll of living cities. The date of the great battle of Talikot is given in various chronograms. One says "Victory of religion and death of the accursed," from which the letters give the date A.H. 972 (A.D. 1564-5). Another is given by Ferishta, "Murder of Ramraj," which, he says, gives, after the subtraction of one letter equivalent to 3, A.H. 972. Nizam Shah is said to have sent the head of Ramraj as a significant warning to Imad-ul-Mulk who had been plundering his districts.

Ali obtained possession, by this victory, of the forts of Raichor and Madgal, and, after enforcing his authority over these places, and leaving them in proper hands, he returned to Bijapur, where, with the wealth he had obtained in the general plunder of Vijayanagar he began, and carried out, that most necessary and desirable work—the walling in, and fortification of, the whole city of Bijapur. Hitherto the only completely defended portion of the capital was the citadel, but a great town had grown up around it which was completely at the mercy of an invader. This undertaking was completed in A.H. 973 (A.D. 1565).

The avarice of Ali Adil Shah led him to think of following up the defeat of Ramraj by an attack on Palganda, and for this purpose he despatched an army under Kishwar Khan to invade the south. Kutub Shah, becoming jealous of his continued acquisitions of territory, and fearing his power might eventually become so great that there would be no withstanding him, induced Nizam Shah to join him in seizing upon this opportunity, when his troops were away in the south, to sweep down upon Bijapur and take the pride out of Ali Adil Shah. Accordingly they marched against the city, and were beginning to make themselves very disagreeable, when, in the midst of an attack made on the enemy by Ali Adil Shah, a cloud of dust was seen to rise on the southern horizon. Presently the outline of a considerable body of horse was discerned, in full gallop towards Bijapur, and, while both sides were wondering whether it was friend or foe, Kishwar Khan, with 20,000 horse, dashed headlong into the enemy's ranks and scattered them. This surprise completely upset them, and many prisoners were taken, amongst them being Molana Inayat Ulla, a near relative of Nizam Shah. Ali Adil Shah sent a respectful message to Nizam Shah telling him that he did not wish to push matters further, but that he could not be responsible for the actions of Kishwar Khan, who was bent on revenge, and he advised him to return to his home. Thinking prudence the better part of valour, Nizam Shah complied; but as soon as he felt himself on his legs again, he once more essayed to try results with Bijapur. Kishwar Khan proceeded against him, but, owing to dissensions among his officers, the enemy overcame the Bijapur troops and Kishwar Khan himself was killed. Ali Adil Shah was thus obliged to take the field in person and retrieve the lost honours of war. After this, an expedition under Ankas Khan marched against and captured Adoni. Then Ali Adil Shah made an unsuccessful raid against Palganda which he had to abandon.

During the reigns of Yusaf, Ismail, and Ibrahim I., the Bijapur troops had been brought into contact with a new power on the coast. Goa, and the coast districts, had fallen to the lot of Yusaf Adil Shah on his revolt, it having been, up to that time, an outlying province of the Bahmani kingdom. A fleet had been collected that used to cruise along these shores, and these ships Vasco da Gama came into contact with when he came in sight of the Indian coast in 1498. He evidently had a brush with them, for it is said he took its commander, a Spanish Jew, prisoner. In 1510 Affonso de Albuquerque arrived before Goa with a great fleet, and, after some resistance on the part of the Bijapur troops, took possession of it, and entered it in great triumph. Three months after this, a strong expedition was despatched from Bijapur, which soon drove the Portuguese back to their ships ; but before the year was out, the latter, strengthened by a fresh squadron from Europe, appeared once more before the fort, and taking it by assault, drove the king's troops from the city with great slaughter. Annoyed by the part the Muhammandans of the city had played in turning about from one side to the other as suited their purpose, Albuquerque set loose his soldiers upon them and spared neither man, woman, or child. One of the most fearful massacres recorded in the annals of Indian history, accompanied with the most barbarous cruelty, then ensued. He put the city in a thorough state of defence and overhauled its forts, turrets, and bastions, repairing them where necessary. In 1570 the kings of the Dekhan combined in an attempt to oust the Portuguese. Ali Adil Shah with 100,000 men and 2,140 elephants besieged the city for ten months but was in the end obliged to retire.

Ali Adil Shah, after this, marched against the forts of Torgal, Dharwar, and Bankapur, wresting them from the feudal chiefs nominally under the orders of the brother of Ramraj. Leaving Mustafa Khan in charge of Bankapur, and reinstating the other chiefs as his own vassals, he returned to Bijapur.

In a dispute with a slave from Gulburgah, regarding the return of certain jewels which had belonged to his daughter, Ali Adil Shah was struck in the bowels with a dagger, from the effect of which he immediately died. This happened in A.H. 988 (A.D. 1580), and he was buried in a very plain looking tomb in the south-west corner of the city. Many works of utility are ascribed to him, among which are the walls around the city; the Gagan Mahal, 1561; the Chand Bauri; the great Jami Masjid, which was left well in hand; the Anand Mahal; and his own tomb. On one of the bastions of the fort of Raichor is an inscription of his reign recording the building of the same by Tahir Khan in A.H. 978 (A.D. 1570). In it Ali's full name and title are given as Abu Al-Muzaffar A'li A'adil-Shah.* He

*Indian Antiquary, Vol. XI., page 130.

built the fort of Shahadrug under the supervision of Mir Naimat Ulla in 966 (A.D. 1558). The suburb of Shahapur was laid out under Kishwar Khan in 967 (A.D. 1559). He built the Harya Mahal in 968 (A.D. 1560); the fort of Dharwar in A.H. 975 (A.D. 1567); the forts of Shahanur and Bankapur in A.H. 981 (A.D. 1573); and he laid out the Bara Imam and Fadk gardens in A.D. 974 and 976 (A.D. 1566 and 1568) respectively. A chronogram gives the date of his death in the Persian equivalent of the words "He saw oppression," A.H. 988.

Ibrahim (II.) Adil Shah; 1580—1626.—Immediately upon the news of Adil Shah's death becoming known, there was great alarm and confusion in the city. The nobles gathered in groups and whispered their misgivings, and eagerly questioned one another as to what was about to happen. The king had left no issue, and it was doubtful who should succeed him. By common consent they appealed to Afzal Khan, who convened a meeting of some of the leading men with the result that they decided that the young Ibrahim, the king's nephew, and son of his brother Tahmasp, was the next of kin, and should be installed as king. Accordingly, and without further loss of time, Ibrahim was brought forth, was seated upon the *masnad*, and the royal umbrella was raised above him. Here he received the salutations of the people and was hailed as king Ibrahim II. He was generally called Ibrahim Jagat Gir (Ibrahim, the holder of the world).

Kamil Khan, an officer of high standing, took upon himself the chief power and care of the state, the king being but a child of nine years of age. But with his power grew his ambition and avarice, and, as with others before him, he soon committed the fatal error of aspiring to powers that were vested in the king alone. He began to use the treasury as he thought fit, and he is charged with having transferred much of its contents to his own coffers. He became daily more arrogant, harsh, and overbearing, and was even most uncivil to the widowed Queen, Chand Bibi.

Resenting his rude conduct, she set about to devise means for his removal, and she was seconded in her efforts by those who were tired of Kamil Khan's behaviour. She sent a woman's dress and a spinning wheel to Kishwar Khan, and commanded him either to rid them of this man or to don this dress and sit at the wheel. Kishwar Khan, stung to action by this taunt, went off at once with a company of desperadoes in seach of Kamil Khan. They found him superintending a building that was in progress, and, as they advanced towards him, he, suspecting their intentions, climbed over and dropped from the wall into the ditch. He succeeded in reaching his house, and, taking all the money and jewels he could carry, fled from the city in the direction of Gulburgah. On finding that Kamil Khan had left the city, Kishwar Khan sent armed men in pursuit, who, coming up with him four or five miles from the gates, plundered him and brought back his head. He had been in power but a little over two months when his punishment overtook him.

A consultation now took place between Kishwar Khan, Murtuza Khan, Anju, Shah Kasim, Ghalib Khan, and Motbar Khan, leading men of the city, about the appointment of a successor to Kamil Khan. Words ran high and a general quarrel took place; weapons were drawn, a free fight ensued, and blood was shed within the palace. Kishwar Khan is said to have pressed the acceptance of the office upon Afzal Khan who had hitherto kept aloof from these broils, but in reality he assumed the full powers of the same himself. Nizam Shah and Kutub Shah, taking advantage of this state of affairs, found a pretext for marching against Bijapur. Kishwar Khan urged Afzal Khan to lead the troops against them. Afzal Khan thereupon joined the army with several of the leading nobles, and leading it first against Kutub Shah, and then against Nizam Shah, succeeding in defeating both. News now reach the camp of the evil doings of Kishwar Khan at home. The nobles in camp unitedly wrote to Chand Bibi, and she advised that Mustafa Khan, Governor of Bankapur, should be called to the capital and appointed in the place of Kishwar Khan. The latter, hearing, of this, at once sent a small force off under Amin Khan against Mustafa Khan. They stormed and took Bankapur and compelled him to flee for protection to another fort under a Hindu chief; but, just as he was being hoisted up over the walls by a rope let down for that purpose he was seized and murdered. Chand Bibi, much incensed at the cowardly action of Kishwar Khan, charged him with treachery; but, having become more impudent and daring than ever, now that his rival was removed, he had the Queen sent in custody to Satara and there imprisoned.

When this news reached the army in the field, Ikhlas Khan, with a large force, immediately marched to Bijapur. Kishwar Khan, not having a sufficient body of men at command to oppose him, gathered up his valuables and made for Ahmednagar. Here, having heard of his perfidious behaviour, they would have nothing to do with him and drove him from the place. He then entered the territory of Kutub Shah, where he was identified by a man of Mustafa Khan's household, who murdered him, and thus avenged the death of his master. Kishwar Khan's power had only lasted over a period of four months when he met with the fate of his predecessor.

One of the first acts of Ikhlas Khan on his arrival at the capital was to send and release Chand Bibi and have her brought back to Bijapur. Ikhlas Khan was appointed to the guardianship of the young king, and Rafi-ul-din, cousin of Afzal Khan, still held charge of the treasury. It was found that Kishwar Khan had carried off the royal seal, so business had to be transacted with a substitute found in the treasury, until after a short time, a slave of Kishwar Khan arrived with the original from Golcondah. Ikhlas Khan determined to hand over the wives and children of Kishwar Khan to the sweepers and shoemakers, but the more humane Rafi-ul-din pleaded hard on their behalf, and succeeded in saving them this disgrace.

Taking advantage of the state of anarchy

now prevailing at Bijapur, and the fact that the army was dispersed in different directions—part under Afzal Khan in the north, part away on the expedition that was sent against Mustafa Khan, and the rest retained by Kishwar Khan at the capital for his own purposes—the ever restless king of Ahmednagar, conjointly with Kutub Shah, again invaded Bijapur territory. Afzal Khan finding himself too weak to oppose the combined forces fell back on Bijapur. At this time a general scramble was going on among the nobles of Bijapur, accompanied with bloodshed and imprisonments, for possession of the higher offices of state, and more especially for that of *Vakil*. So much engaged were they with these troubles in the city that no resistance was offered to the enemy in the field, and Bhozad-ul-Mulk brought up a force and invested Bijapur. During these troubles within, Afzal Khan was arrested, imprisoned, and eventually put to death; Rafi-ul-din was also imprisoned, and Shah Abul Hassan was appointed Vakil. Dilawar Khan and Hamid Khan were also appointed to high offices. There were only 3,000 horse in the city, but, notwithstanding this, the enemy without could make little impression upon it, and so confined themselves to the plundering and the destruction of the suburbs. At length the rains came on and the confederate forces, seeing it was useless remaining as they were, raised the siege and returned to their own homes. The management of the state was now entirely in the hands of the Abyssinian nobles who dispersed the Dekhanis by sending them off to take charge of the various forts and other military stations throughout the kingdom.

Kutub Shah, however, renewed the war by sending an army under Mir Zanjbil Istrabadi against Bijapur. Dilavar Khan was selected to take the field against him, and was so succesful, that he routed the enemy and followed him up to the gates of Golcondah, capturing 120 elephants, with horses and other booty. Ikhlas Khan, who remained at the capital in charge of the home troops, now coveted the position held by Dilawar Khan, and to be enabled to gain it without opposition, he induced the king to send an order to Dilawar Khan instructing him to remain in the field until further orders. He also sent orders to Dilawar Khan to send in all the elephants and other booty. This gave the latter great offence, and, suspecting Ikhlas Khan's manœuvres, he marched rapidly on Bijapur. In the meanwhile a quarrel had taken place between Ikhlas Khan and Hamid Khan about the possession of an elephant. Ikhlas Khan accused Hamid Khan of unlawful possession of an elephant, while the latter accused the former of having possessed himself, illegally, of certain districts and land. Hamid Khan was seconded by Dilawar Khan and Haidar Khan, and Ikhlas Khan, finding argument of no avail, gathered together troops and guns before the citadel which he forthwith began to besiege. He was opposed by the others, and for several days fighting was carried on around the citadel gate. Other nobles, not implicated in this quarrel, tried to bring about a reconciliation, but, owing to the ill nature of Ikhlas Khan, their efforts were of no avail. Thus the quarrel was kept up for two months, when Ikhlas Khan, getting the worst of the situation, and being deserted by most of his men, came to terms and returned to his home. Dilawar Khan now advised him to make a pilgrimage to Makka, and Ikhlas Khan, seeing the futility of remaining any longer in Bijapur, agreed, and set out on his journey; but as soon as he reached the fort of Murtazabad (Miraj) he was immediately imprisoned and blinded. Subsequently king Ibrahim granted him a *jaghir* for his maintenance, which he enjoyed until 1597 when he died.

Abul Hassan had been ousted and Dilawar Khan now held the reins. Hamid Khan was a quiet man and much averse to quarrels, so he offered little opposition to the designs of his friend; but, nevertheless, a feeling of uneasiness beset him, and he watched the intrigues of Dilawar Khan with great anxiety. This strained relationship, led to ill feeling and eventually to the imprisonment of Hamid Khan and confiscation of all his propertv.

Dilawar Khan now ruled alone, but though cruel to his friend, to his credit it is recorded that he ruled well and wisely. He caused Abul Hassan, whom he had imprisoned, to be blinded and put to death. His four sons were well provided for, and to each was given the command of 2,000 troops. In this manner did Dilawar Khan make himself secure, and he materially curtailed the power and influence of Chand Bibi. The king himself was even obedient and submissive to him, and consequently feared him. In order to improve the relationship between Bijapur and the states of Ahmednagar and Golcondah, Dilawar Khan brought about the marriage of Ibrahim's sister, Khadijah Sultana, with the son of Murtaza Nizam Shah, and that of the daughter of Kutub Shah with Ibrahim Adil Shah.

It seems to have occurred to Dilawar Khan about this time to dethrone Ibrahim and place his brother Ismail, who was imprisoned in the fort of Mustafabad, on the throne in his place. This came to the ears of the king and his foster mother, and soon became known to the general public. Most of the nobles, and the bulk of the populace, were so indignant at this that they but awaited the slightest hint from the king to wreak their vengence upon Dilawar Khan; and he, being fearful for his life, confined himself for several days to his own house, not daring to show himself in public. On sending a message of great humility to the king, and pretending that he was very wrongfully used, in being unreasonably suspected of evil designs against his person, the latter softened towards him, and had him escorted with honour to the palace, when they became, for a time, reconciled. Dilawar Khan now began to provide against a future emergency of this sort by increasing his own troops. To these he added five or six thousand horsemen, and the king was induced to give over considerable bodies of his own troops to the command of Dilawar Khan's sons.

About this time a disagreement ensued between Burhan Shah and his brother Murtuza Nizam Shah of Ahmednagar, which resulted in the former seeking the assistance of Raja Ali Khan of Burhanpur and Ibrahim Adil Shah. Jamal Khan, the chief of the Ahmednagar army, had conceived a plan to set up Ismail, the son of Burhan Shah, upon the throne. Ibrahim and Dilawar Khan set out to assist Burhan Shah, but were met by Jamal Khan who at first tried to come to terms with them. Dilawar Khan would hear of nothing short of taking Jamal Khan prisoner; and, against the advice of Ibrahim, he advanced against him. At the outset he was successful, notwithstanding the treachery of Ain-ul-Mulk and Ankas Khan who deserted him at the last moment; but whilst his troops were dispersed and engaged in plunder, the enemy, rallying round their prince Ismail, returned to the charge and compelled him to fly. Dilawar, on joining the King, urged him to retreat with all haste to Shahadrug. On arrival they found all their property and munitions of war, which had been left there for safety, had been plundered, so they were obliged to send to Bijapur for fresh stores to replace them.

Jamal Khan, after returning to Ahmednagar for fresh material of war, set out to attack Burhan Shah in Berar. On this Dilawar Khan despatched a considerable body of horse to worry Jamal Khan when he should be engaged with Burhan Shah, but Jamal Khan, getting news of this move, hurried on to give battle to Burhan Shah, before the Bijapur horse should arrive. An action ensued, and Burhan Shah was getting into difficulties when Dilawar Khan's horse arrived and turned the fortunes of the day. Jamal Khan fell in this action, being pierced by an arrow. Burhan Shah at once repaired to Ahmednagar, where he had himself proclaimed king, and sent Ismail into confinement in the fortress of Lohargarh.

Dilawar Khan was blamed for the very heavy losses occasioned by this campaign; and Ibrahim, wearying of his yoke, began to plan means of ridding himself of it. He sent an obscure Hindu servant to Ain-ul-Mulk and Ankas Khan, telling them that he was pretty well disgusted with the arrogance of Dilawar Khan, and would gladly avail himself of their assistance if they would continue to be loyal to him as their forefathers had been to his house before him. At midnight the king left his palace, and, with a few trusty followers, went over to the camp of Ain-ul-Mulk. In the morning, Dilawar Khan, counting upon the attachment of the rest of the nobles to him, imagined they would, at his command, immediately give up the king; and on this assumption he proceeded with great pomp to where the king was, and insolently demanded of him by whose authority he had left the palace. The king, without answering him, and feeling greatly incensed at his conduct, ordered one of his men to chastise him. This man, flourishing his sword, struck him from his horse. Dilawar Khan was wounded, but not fatally, aud was at once removed by his men. Seeing there was no chance for him at Bijapur, he fled to Bidar and thence to Ahmednagar, where it is said he was received with honour, and was given a high post in the public works department of the state.

Those men, who were now disappointed in not getting the appointments they wished, began to work mischief between Ahmednagar and Bijapur, with the result that Burhan Nizam Shah sent an army against Bijapur. Dilawar Khan accompanied this force, and they met the Bijapur troops on the banks of the Bhanorah. Here Dilawar Khan sent a very humble message to king Ibrahim promising to come back if he would give him a deed guaranteeing his life and property. This the king granted, and Dilawar Khan came back to Bijapur with the secret intention of revenging himself upon the king when he again got into power. But cunning was met with cunning, and the king no sooner had him in his hands than he blinded and imprisoned him in the fort of Satara, telling him he promised him his life and property and he had kept his promise. Dilawar Khan was then upwards of eighty years of age, and he is said to have lived ten years longer in confinement before he died.

Ibrahim now directed his attention to Burhan Nizam Shah who had taken up a strong position on the river Bhima. Rumi Khan was despatched with an army against him, and was soon confronted by Nur Khan Dekhani with 12,000 horse. A battle was fought, when Nizam Shah's force gave way and finally fled, leaving in the hands of the victors 160 elephants, a great number of horses, and other booty. Burhan Nizam Shah now sought peace, but Ibrahim only consented to it on the former destroying the fortified position he had established on the

Bhima. Burhan Shah next tampered with Ain-ul-Mulk and Ankas Khan, who were already estranged from their king, and induced them to take up the cause of Ismail, brother of Ibrahim, and to proclaim him king. The plan was put in hand, and Ain-ul-Mulk and his colleague, professing the greatest loyalty to Ibrahim, were secretly winning over others to their side. Eventually, when the plot was considered ripe for execution, they liberated Ismail from his imprisonment at Belgaum, seized the fort, and proclaimed him king. Ibrahim despatched Alyas Khan with troops to quell this disturbance; but when the latter found that both Ain-ul-Mulk and Ankas Khan were among the rebels, and that they had become too powerful to be successfully opposed with the handful of troops he had brought with him, he returned to Bijapur. The king now freed Hamid Khan, whom Dilawar Khan imprisoned. Hamid Khan set out for the scene of the disturbance (1594), and, as he neared the army of the Pretender, he sent a message to Ain-ul-Mulk telling him he had escaped from Bijapur, and, with his troops, was coming to join their camp. Deceived by this, Ain-ul-Mulk made great preparations to receive Hamid Khan with honour. In this way the latter was allowed to march close up to the camp, his men being on the alert for their leader's signal. Ain-ul-Mulk's army, thrown off their guard by the magnificent arrangements for the reception of Hamid Khan, were suddenly aroused to the real state of affairs by an unexpected discharge of Hamid Khan's artillery in their midst. All was confusion in an instant, and, as Ain-ul-Mulk was endeavouring to rally his troops, he was knocked off his horse and was subsequently beheaded. Ismail was taken prisoner, blinded, and placed in strict confinement where he soon sickened and died. The army of Ahmednagar, which was coming to the assistance of the rebels, had proceeded a short distance on their way, when, hearing of this defeat, they returned. Hamid Khan marched back to Bijapur in triumph, where honours and distinction awaited him at his sovereign's hand.

Burhan Nizam Shah, soon after this, was taken suddenly ill, and, calling Ibrahim, his eldest son, to his side, proclaimed him his heir. On his death, Ibrahim, was duly proclaimed king, and he at once proceeded to wreak vengeance on the king of Bijapur for having defeated his father. Ibrahim Adil Shah moved out against him, and an action took place, in which Ibrahim Nizam Shah was killed, having been shot through the shoulders with an arrow. The Ahmednagar forces fled, and the Bijapur troops returned to Shahadrug where Ibrahim Adil Shah had awaited them. Thence they proceeded together to Bijapur, having halted awhile on the banks of the Bhima on account of the Muhurram, and entered the city amidst great rejoicings. The streets were profusely decorated and brilliantly illuminated. Ibrahim entered his capital on the 14th Muhurram 1004 (A.D. 1595) and proceeded to the Anand Mahal where he distributed rewards and addressed his troops. He now applied himself to business, and was very assiduous in its execution, attending many hours daily in public darbar, where he heard and disposed of petitions, and dispensed justice to the poor. All were well pleased with his rule, and none were able to find fault with it.

Great dissensions now arose among the nobles of Ahmednagar. Manju Khan had taken possession of the fort and treasury, and had thus aroused the ill-feelings of the other nobles. This culminated in a skirmish between the Habshis and Dekhanis, resulting in a victory for the former. Manju Khan now wrote to the prince Shah Murad, son of Akbar Padshah, to come with all haste and take over the fort of Ahmednagar. The prince was not slow to use this favourable opportunity of gaining a footing in the Dekhan, and accordingly started off towards the city. But before he arrived Manju Khan had overcome the Habshis, and, not needing his assistance any longer, now refused to give up the fort. Upon this Murad surrounded it, when Manju Khan, who was nobly seconded in his efforts by Chand Bibi, applied to Bijapur for help. Ibrahim at first sent Rafi-ul-din to Shahadrug, and thence to Ahmednagar to try and reconcile the nobles, who were still holding aloof from one another, and to induce them to combine against their common enemy. Chand Bibi had made the journey from Bijapur to Ahmednagar with her niece, Khadijah Sultana, on the occasion of the marriage of the latter to Murtaza Nizam Shah, and she never afterwards returned. Rafi-ul-din succeeded in bringing about a better feeling, but it did not last long, and very soon all was in confusion again. Chand Bibi, who was at the head of the party confined to the fort, despairing of the assistance ever arriving which she had asked from Ibrahim Adil Shah, was obliged to come to terms with the Mughals by ceding the Berars to them.

In the year 1008 (A.D. 1599) Ibrahim determined to remove the seat of government from Bijapur to a more pleasant spot four miles out to the west. There he began to build a new city, and ordered his nobles and all the leading merchants of the town to construct their residences and places of business there. The public works generally, with the construction of royal palaces and the fortifications, were entrusted to Nawab Shavaz Khan. It is said that upwards of 20,000 artizans and labourers were gathered together for this new venture, and it was Ibrahim's wish to build such a city as would not have its equal in Hindustan. Money was freely lent from the treasury to those who wished to build, and soon great rivalry sprang up among the nobles in their attempts to outdo one another in the erection of their palaces. The new city was called Nauraspur; but its progress was suddenly interrupted, tradition says, by the astrologers who warned the king that if he removed from Bijapur it would be attended with evil results. Another account tells us that the new city continued to increase, and was well populated and adorned with public and other buildings, up to the year 1034 (A.D. 1634) when Malik Ambar came down upon Bijapur with sixty thousand horse. He plundered and destroyed the suburbs together with Nauraspur, whose walls and fortifications had not been completed; and from that year Ibrahim, having all his works destroyed, abandoned the idea of a new city.

When Akbar penetrated into the Dekhan and besieged Ahmednagar, he sent such a message to Ibrahim, as is said to have astounded the Bijapur court, regarding the non-payment of the annual tribute. But matters were soon placed on a more satisfactory footing by the betrothal of Sultana Begam, Ibrahim's daughter, to prince Danial. The marriage, however, did not take place until Danial returned from Burhanpur to Ahmednagar some five years later; but in the same year he died from excessive drinking.

Malik Ambar placed Murtaza Nizam Shah on the throne, and proceeded, with the assistance of troops from Bijapur, against the Mughals. The Dekhanis eventually succeeded in driving them out of the fort of Ahmednagar and took possession of it themselves. There now followed frequent quarrels between Murtaza Nizam Shah and Malik Ambar, and it was only by the intervention of Ibrahim, who pointed out to them the danger of party disputes while the enemy was watching his opportunity to pounce upon them, that they were pacified. Malik Ambar, although so frequently assisted by Ibrahim, grew so intoxicated with his successes that his behaviour became very over-bearing and offensive. Ibrahim determined to bring him to his senses, and despatched an army against him, which in a pitched battle, was defeated. This was in

1033 (A.D. 1623). Next year Malik Ambar followed up his victory by invading Bijapur territory and carrying destruction and desolation up to the very walls of the capital. Nauraspur, not yet completely walled in, fell an easy prey to his arms, and was plundered and ruined. Malik Ambar died in the following year (A.D. 1625) before Ibrahim could rally sufficiently to take revenge upon him.

Ibrahim contracted a very serious disease which his own physicians could not cure. He then summoned an European physician, who was at Bijapur, named Farna Lup. This man tried to treat him, but was not successful, and the king died. It is said that the king's servants ascribed his death to the treatment of this European, whom they caught and disfigured by cutting off his nose and upper lip. Farna Lup immediately replaced the detached members, and in a short time they grew again in their old places. This clever bit of surgery raised him at once in the estimation of the citizens, and soon restored him to former favour.

Ibrahim died on the 10th Muharram 1037 (A.D. 1627). He left four sons, *viz.*, Darvesh Padshah, born of Malika Jahan; Sultan Suliman, born of Kamal Khatun; Sultan Muhammad, born of Taj Sultana; and the infant son of Sundar Mahal. Sultan Muhammad succeeded him. It is said the king was handsome, liberal, and careful about his subjects. He patronized learning and the fine arts, and was passionately fond of music and singing; and it is said that it was due to the company of Hindu musicians and singers that he imbibed his liking for, and leanings towards, certain Hindu deities with the worship of which he has been charged. During his reign, a saint name Hazrat Shah Subgat Ulla arrived from Medina, and was so shocked at the debauchery he saw carried on in the city, that heseverely reprimanded Ibrahim for it. He promised to give him three kingdoms if he would but comply with three requests. The first was that he should abolish all the liquor shops in the town, the second that he should compel all women of loose character to be married, and the third that he should give no public office to a man of the Rafzi (Shiah) faith. This was too much for the king; so, at the advice of his minister, he gave the saint leave to the depart from the city.

During his reign were built the Sat Khanka Mahal (Sat Manjli), in 1583; the Haidar Burj in the same year; the Malika Jahan Masjid in 1587; the Anand Mahal, for dancing and singing in, in 1589; and the Sangat or Nauras Mahal, and other buildings in Nauraspur, from 1599 to 1624.

Muhammad Kasim Ferishta, the great Muhammadan historian, lived and wrote his works during Ibrahim's reign, and for the next three kings we have but scanty records.

Sultan Muhammad, 1627—1655.—Although Darvesh Padshah was the eldest son of Ibrahim, yet he was set aside in favour of Muhammad who was only fifteen years old when he was called to the *masnad*. This was brought about chiefly by one of the ministers named Daulat Khan, who falsely proclaimed it as king Ibrahim's wish. Darvesh was blinded and Suliman maimed, by which means they were both rendered unfit to succeed to the throne. The day following the king's death Muhammad was placed upon the *masnad,* and the nobles and citizens came with their *nazzars* to do obeisance to the new king. Mirza Muhammad Amin Lari was given the title of Mustafa Khan, while to Daulat Khan was given that of Khawas Khan.

One of Muhammad's first acts was to march into Ahmednagar territory, in the direction of the fort Kes-Darur, bent upon conquest. He was met by Nizam Shah's forces and defeated them. Nizam Shah's army under Hamid Khan now invaded Bijapur territory. Muhammad despatched a force under Nawab Khan Baba, Ikhlas Khan, and Itmad Khan, which meeting the enemy at Kanvar, engaged and dispersed them. On this the Ahmednagar troops withdrew to their own territory. Whilst this was going on, news was received of the rebellion of Kadam Rao, governor of Bijapur. A force under Mir Ali Raza was sent against him, which eventually broke up the rebellion, and Kadam Rao was taken prisoner and executed.

Ibrahim Adil Shah was much incensed against Ahmednagar on account of the destruction of Nauraspur, but did not live to carry out his intention of retaliation. Mustafa Khan, however, burned for revenge, more especially as his own father-in-law, Baba Khan, had been executed by Malik Ambar. He wished to overrun the country with the assistance of the Mughals and to divide it with them. Khawas Khan opposed this idea as a foolish action which would strengthen the hands of the Mughals, who would then, perhaps, turn about on Bijapur. Mustafa Khan's counsel, however, prevailed, and an army was sent to the assistance of the Mughals. This led to bitter enmity between Khawas Khan and Mustafa Khan. As feared by Khawas Khan, Shah Jahan soon broke off his treaty relations with Bijapur, and sent a force into that district, which marched up to the very city itself and encamped outside the walls near the tank of the dyers. They were repulsed, and the Bijapur troops, under Murari, followed them up as far as Parandah. It was while he was at Parandah that Murari received orders from the king to bring away the Malik-i-Maidan to Bijapur, which was on the fort there. This was in 1632.

A fresh Mughal army set out from Burhanpur towards Daulatabad. This fort was then held by an Ahmednagar officer, Fateh Khan, who had the young king Husain Nizam Shah with him. The fort was closely invested by the Mughals, and, at length, Fateh Khan, whose provisions had run short, was obliged to call on Muhammad Shah to assist him. Seeing the mistake they had made in assisting the Mughals at the outset, the Bijapur nobles at once despatched a force under Murari with provisions to Fateh Khan's relief. Murari, instead of carrying out his mission, for some reason delayed to assist the besieged, and, being starved out, Fateh Khan was obliged to surrender the fort with his own person and that of the king Husain Shah. Husain Shah was imprisoned in the fortress of Gwalior, and, from this time, the Nizam Shahi kingdom ceased to exist.

There was now a scramble for the division of the Ahmednagar kingdom. Siddi Rehan collected men at Sholapur, Shaji Bhosle made himself secure at Bhimgadh, Satvas Rao at Junner, Sidi Saba and Sef Khan took possession of the Konkan, and Siddi Ambar possessed himself of the island of Rajpuri. Other killadars and zamindars seized upon whatever districts or forts they had charge of, and soon everything was in an utter state of confusion. In the midst of all this Shaji released Murtaza, a descendant of the Nizam Shahi family, from the fort of Jivdhan, and, at the fort of Bhimgadh, had him installed as king, thereby thinking to serve his own ends in his ambitious designs upon the Ahmednagar territory.

Mahabat Khan, after the fall of Daulatabad, returned to the attack of Parandah, which was held by Bijapur troops under Randaulah Khan, but he was unable to effect anything, and returned to Burhanpur.

Khawas Khan, getting Mustafa Khan into his power, imprisoned him in the fort of Belgaum, and thereby evoked the severe displeasure of Muhammad Shah, who henceforth took a great dislike to Khawas Khan, and was bent upon his ruin. The rest of the nobles, beginning to fear the tyranny of Khawas Khan and his friend Murari, seceded in a body to Gulburgah. They had been further incensed against him on hearing that he had written to Shah Jahan, telling him the nobles were in rebellion, and calling upon him for assistance, promising to hand over to him the city of Badyapur (Bijapur).

The increasing power of Shaji, and the failure of Mahabat Khan at Parandah, brought the emperor Shah Jahan again to the Dekhan.

He divided his army into two portions, one to act against Shaji, while the other was directed against Bijapur. Muhammad Shah, unable to meet the imperial troops in the field, shut himself up within the city, destroyed all forage and provisions for twenty miles around Bijapur, which he was not able to take into the capital, emptied the tanks, and left the country so barren and desolate that it was impossible for an army to remain long in it. Thus thwarted in their attack on Bijapur the enemy confined themselves to the plunder and destruction of the towns and villages in the surrounding districts. Seeing that he could not save the country from ruin, Muhammad sued for peace. This was granted; and, in return for an annual tribute to Delhi of twenty lakhs, he was allowed to hold the forts of Sholapur and Parandah, with a portion of the Ahmednagar dominions, the country between the Bhima and Nira rivers, and the whole of the Konkan. He was also to abstain from assisting Shaji, but the latter was soon reduced to submission, was pardoned, and given a command in the Bijapur service.

During the period which succeeded, from 1636 to the death of Muhammad in 1656, Bijapur enjoyed comparative immunity from troubles without or within; and the king used this time in completing his own gigantic mausoleum, and erecting many other buildings throughout the city. Under the superintendence of Afzal Khan, the water supply to the city was considerably increased by a conduit from a fresh source, the Begam Talao, to the south of the town. Muhammad built the Asar Mahal as a Hall of Justice, but it was subsequently used as a repository for the sacred relics—the two hairs of Muhammad's beard—which are still safe within its walls. In 1641 Muhammad married the daughter of the king of Golcondah.

Shaji was now employed as one of the Bijapur chiefs in the Karnatic. He possessed his heriditary estate near Poona, where he had left his wife Jiji Bai, a most ambitious woman, and his son Sivaji. As the latter grew up, a restless and adventurous character, fired with an ambition to found a Maratha kingdom, he gradually gathered around him associates willing to share his fortunes in his enterprises, and eventually became strong enough to take possession of several of the old forts of the Western Ghats, pretending to do so in the name of the king. But having intercepted some government treasure, and committed other highhanded offences, he was denounced as a rebel, and his father Shaji was recalled and imprisoned on the suspicion of being concerned in his son's misdoings.

Prince Aurangzib returned in 1650 to his government of the Dekhan; very soon got mixed up with the affairs of Golcondah; and marched against it with his troops. While here, the news arrived of the death of Muhammad in the year 1656.

Ali (II.) Adil Shah, 1656—1672.—The treaty by which Bijapur remitted an annual tax to Delhi constituted, in the eyes of Shah Jahan, a reason for interfering in its affairs, and controlling it, to a certain extent, as a tributary state. Great offence was thus given to the emperor by the succession of Ali Adil Shah without any previous reference to him, and he accordingly seized upon the opportunity for active interference. He denounced Ali as spurious, and contended that Muhammad had no male offspring, and hence the state had lapsed to the empire for want of a legitimate heir. Bernier, a French physician, who lived for some years at the court of Aurangzib, says, Muhammad died without leaving male issue, and Ali was a youth whom his queen, sister of the king of Golcondah, had adopted as a son. Ali, who was only nineteen years old, indignantly repudiated these charges, and absolutely refused to submit to the orders of the emperor. Aurangzib, who appears to have been concocting plans for the reduction and partition of Bijapur with the traitor Mir Jumlah, immediately marched from Golcondah to Bijapur, laying waste and ravaging the country as he proceeded, and laid siege to the capital. The Bijapur army in the field was bought over by Aurangzib and ceased to molest the invaders, while, within the city, factions were at variance with each other. But as the siege proceeded, and the danger increased, party spirit for a time was laid aside, and all united in offering a stubborn resistance to the Mughals. Aurangzib, in his desire for the dissolution of the Bijapur kingdom, would not listen to the king's call for terms, but insisted upon complete and unconditional surrender. But just as the outlook to the besieged was beginning to appear very gloomy, Aurangzib got news of his father's serious illness, and hurried back to Dehli to secure to himself the succession in the event of Shah Jahan's death, having hastily concluded a peace with Bijapur.

Ali Adil Shah was not free for long, however, from troubles from without. Sivaji, who had thrown off all allegiance to Bijapur, had been favourably backed, in his ever increasing aggressions, by the Mughals. On the departure of Aurangzib, Khan Muhammad, who was remaining inactive in the field with his troops while Aurangzib was besieging Bijapur, was induced to return to the city, but he had hardly entered by the Makka gate when he was dragged from his elephant and killed. Some ascribe this act to the instigation of the king, others say it was the work of a private enemy. Sivaji was now making things very unpleasant for Bijapur; he was plundering and raiding in Bijapur territory, and carrying on a predatory warfare against Dekhanis and Mughals alike, only intent upon setting up a kingdom for himself and exterminating the unclean Moslem. It was decided to send out an expedition against him and bring him to his senses. Afzal Khan was selected as the commander of the army in succession to Khan Muhammad, and, when all was ready, he set out for Sivaji's retreat. Before leaving the capital it is said that the astrologers warned Afzal Khan that he was starting upon a fatal expedition from which he would never return alive; and so impressed was he by this prediction, that he is said to have had his sixty-four wives drowned. At a certain spot, a short distance north of the Torweh road, outside the city on the west, are pointed out seven rows of tombs of females, all symmetrically arranged upon a single platform, which are said to be the graves of his wives; and a well adjoining them is said to be the one in which they met their fate. North of this again is Afzal Khan's own cenotaph, built during his life-time, but unoccupied by him. His bones lie upon the slopes of Partabgarh. But to return. Afzal Khan directed the march of his troops towards Sivaji's stronghold on Partabgarh, where, on his arrival, he was met by men from Sivaji, wh,s on behalf of their chief, professed his complete submission and a desire for a personal interview with Afzal Khan. They induced the latter to lead his troops up into the rugged glens below the fort, and pointed out a suitable place of meeting upon the hillside immediately under the crest. It was agreed that each was to come with only one armed attendant. While this was going on, Sivaji's troops, unseen, were quietly surrounding the Bijapur army. Afzal Khan repaired to the place of rendezvous, where he soon saw Sivaji coming to meet him. As the latter bent forward for the customary embrace, he suddenly plunged a dagger he had secreted on his person into the bowels of Afzal Khan. The Khan tried to defend himself, but he was set on by both Sivaji and his friend Tanaji

Malusray, overpowered, and speedily despatched. At a given signal the hordes of Sivaji swept down from all sides upon the unsuspecting troops they had been eagerly watching from their hiding places, and almost annihilated them. A remnant, only, escaped to Bijapur.

On the news of this disastrous defeat reaching the capital, a new expedition under Fazil Khan, the son of Afzal Khan, was rapidly equipped, but not until Sivaji, following up his advantage, had ravaged the greater parts of the western districts of Bijapur, and had carried plunder and devastation up to the gates of the city itself. The king, himself, also took the field; but, beyond reducing to submission several disaffected chiefs, he made little impression upon Sivaji. On the other hand, the latter grew so powerful and troublesome, that it was deemed advisable later on, in 1662, to come to terms with him, and a treaty was signed by which Sivaji was confirmed in his possession of the whole of the Konkan and a good slice of the Dekhan.

Sivaji could not rest. Bound down to keep the peace with Bijapur, he did not see any reason why he should not try to wrest a few districts from the Mughals. His interference angered Aurangzib, who had by this time succeeded his father on the throne of Dehli, and an army under Raja Jayasingh was sent to the Dekhan to punish this freebooter, and at the same time accomplish the long wished for conquest of Bijapur. Sivaji was soon obliged to come to terms, and he agreed to join the imperial army against Bijapur. The combined forces proceeded to lay siege to the city in 1666. Ali Adil Shah resorted to the old plan of laying waste the country immediately around the capital, so that the invading army would hardly be able to subsist for want of water and forage. The army of Jayasingh soon began to suffer from lack of provisions, and, in addition to this, the Bijapur horse, which kept the field, were ever on the alert to cut off what supplies were forthcoming, and harassed the enemy on every opportunity. Jayasingh was at length obliged to raise the siege and retire to Aurangabad, but he was followed by the king's cavalry and suffered heavily from them on the march. Sivaji was thanked by the emperor for his co-operation, and was invited to Dehli, which invitation he reluctantly accepted ; but, while at the court of Aurangzib, his treatment was such as to make him uneasy and fearful for his life. He escaped from the strict surveillance under which he was kept, and, with but a companion or two, returned by unfrequented ways to the Dekhan.

Ali Adil Shah now began to think it time to come to terms with the emperor since these repeated invasions were becoming serious. Hitherto the yearly tribute had fallen into arrears, and this was a constant excuse for Aurangzib's reprisals. A treaty was entered into by which Bijapur lost much of its possessions in the north, including the fort of Sholapur. An understanding was also come to with Sivaji, who was preparing to levy "chauth," and it was agreed to pay him three lakhs of rupees in consideration of his refraining from the collection of this blackmail.

In 1672 the king died of paralysis, in the thirty-fifth year of his age and after a reign of sixteen years. He had received from his father a kingdom intact and flourishing, but to his son Sikandar, now only five years of age, he left a shattered heritage, shorn of some of its best possessions, by Sivaji on the one hand, and the Mughals on the other. He commenced a mausoleum for himself which, had it been completed, would have been by far the most elegant building in the city, but either because he began it too late in life, or was too often interrupted in its construction, it was never finished, and it now remains, conspicuous upon its lofty basement, one of the finest ruins in the city. He was buried in the vault of the unfinished building, which also contains the tombs of his wife and many others, probably members of his household.

Sikandar Adil Shah, 1672—1686.—Amongst the most troublous periods in Bijapur history, as we have seen, have been those when the crown passed to a minor, and the management of the state into the uncertain hands of a regent. No worse luck could have befallen the state at this time, when its very existence was being seriously threatened by the Mughals, and its peace disturbed by the ever restless and treacherous Sivaji, the notorious truce-breaker. Khawas Khan was left as regent to manage the affairs of the state. He was the son of the traitor Khan Muhammad who was murdered near the Makka gate. Sivaji at once took advantage of the party strife that naturally accompanied the regency and stripped Bijapur of many more of her possessions. He had now become sufficiently powerful to be crowned Maharaja in 1674, and to make treaties with the English Factory at Bombay, who thus acknowledged his position. These troubles were now augmented by the inherent treachery of Khawas Khan, who secretly arranged with the Mughals to hand over the city to the viceroy of the Dekhan, Khan Jahan, and to give the beautiful young princess, the king's sister, in marriage to one of the emperor's sons. According to agreement Khan Jahan's army advanced towards Bijapur from Aurangabad, but, owing to the timely detection of the plot by Abdul Karim, an army was sent out against him, and he was soon obliged to fly, most ignominiously, back to his own provinces. The populace, maddened against Khawas Khan, demanded his blood, and he was forthwith led away and executed. Abdul Karim was now appointed regent.

In 1676 Sivaji set out on a plundering expedition into the south of India and captured the forts of Gingi and Vellore, which were then garrisoned by Bijapur troops; and marching to Golcondah, made a treaty with Kutub Shah for the division of Adil Shah's southern provinces. To prevent this being carried out, Abdul Karim, in the following year, arranged with Dilawar Khan, who had succeeded Khah Jahan, to make a joint attack on Golcondah. But their forces were defeated by the enemy under Mahduna Pant, the Golcondah minister, and were compelled to retreat. Long arrears of pay, which the treasury was not able to meet, had spread discontent and disorder throughout the Bijapur army, so that it was next to impossible to mobilise sufficient troops to meet sudden emergencies. To make matters worse, Abdul Karim fell ill of a dangerous disease ; and, as the Government were unable to meet the demands of pay made upon them, it was arranged that Masud Khan, a rich Abyssinian jaghirdar of Adoni, should be tempted with the offer of the high office of regent on condition of his paying off the arrears of pay due to the army. But Masud Khan did not completely fulfil his part of the contract, and as a result, great numbers of the troops deserted to the Mughals and Marathas, where they were paid better. Masud Khan promised the hand of the Padshah Bibi, the king's sister, to the son of Aurangzib, but afterwards refused to carry out his engagement; whereupon Dilawar Khan, who in the meantime had been censured by the emperor for not having pushed the conquest of Bijapur when he had had the chance, formally demanded that she should be sent to the Mughal camp. The Mughal faction in the city, headed by the resident Mughal envoy, were ready to resort to arms to enforce the demand, when the noble little princess, fearful of the result of non-compliance with the claim, gave herself up of her own accord to save her brother and his kingdom. She was sent with due honour and escort to Aurangzib ; but the Mughals, now well on the war path, were not in the humour to turn back, and in 1679 Bijapur was once again besieged by the imperial army. At this crisis Masud Khan called upon Sivaji for aid, and the latter, only too glad of the smallest pretext for a grand raid over the country, at once proceeded to plunder the Mughal provinces as far as Aurangabad. But Dilavar Khan was not to be drawn aside or deterred from the capture of Bijapur, which was now with him, since he had received his emperor's rebuke, a point of honour; and so closely did he beset the city, that Masud Khan was obliged to send messengers to Sivaji entreating him to return and help him to drive off the besieger. Sivaji turned about with the intention of coming to the aid of the city, when he heard of the rebellion of his own son Sambhaji, and, sending on his army under his general Hambir Rao to the relief of Bijapur, he hurried off to Panhala to see to this new disturbance. Between the two, Dilavar Khan was soon obliged to raise the siege and retreat. Sivaji, shortly after this, arrived at Bijapur and received the Raichor Doab, which was the payment agreed upon for his assistance. In 1680 Sivaji died.

Factions again arose in the city when the enemy withdrew, which caused Masud Khan to throw up the regency and retire to his estate at Adoni, and the management of affairs was taken up by Sherza Khan and Sayyid Makhtum. In 1683 Aurangzib marched out of Delhi, with an immense army, intent upon carrying out himself what his generals had failed in—the complete conquest of the Deccan and overthrow of Bijapur. From Delhi he proceeded to Burhanpur, thence to Aurangabad, and at the same time sent off his sons, Prince Mauzim, and Prince Azim, with separate armies to conquer the still resisting forts in the north and west of the Deccan. Prince Azim laid siege to Sholapur in 1685, and, on its fall, he set out for Bijapur. As on former occasions, party spirit in the capital laid aside its jealousies and animosities on the approach of danger, and the prince was kept at bay, for a time, by the troops under Sherza Khan. Towards the end of the year Prince Azim once again marched forward, and this time the Bijapur troops fell back before him to the capital. Aurangzib, himself, was encamped at Sholapur, whence he despatched supplies to the army; but provisions were beginning to run short, and what was sent off was often intercepted by the Bijapur cavalry, who kept the field and harassed the enemy whenever opportunity offered. Famine threatened the imperial forces, but, soon, an extra large supply, escorted by a strong force, reached their camp from Ahmednagar. The emperor, himself, was at this time superintending operations against Haidarabad, but, finding that he was not likely to progress satisfactorily against either, with his forces divided, made peace with the latter, and began to concentrate the whole strength of his army against Bijapur. When he reached the city, he found his son had already commenced the siege, and, with his own army, he was able to completely surround it. A gallant resistance was made, but the emperor, although his batteries had already made several breaches in the walls, waited patiently, knowing that the garrison would soon be starved out and would capitulate. Nor was he wrong in his anticipations, for, reduced to the last extremity, on the 15th

October 1686, the garrison surrendered. The emperor entered in great state, and proceeded to the Hall of Audience in the citadel, where he received the submission of the nobles, and where the king Sikandar is said to have been brought before him in silver chains. The young king was allowed to remain in Bijapur, and was assigned a lakh of rupees annually for his maintenance; but in three years after the fall of the city he died, and, with him, passed away the last of his race. Thus, after a brilliant career of very nearly two hundred years, the Adil Shahi dynasty became extinct, and the kingdom merged into the great empire of Dehli.

Aurangzib remained for some years in the city, during which time a severe plague visited it, which, among its many victims, carried off his queen. She was buried in the enclosure known as the Begam Rauza in the Nau Bag. In 1717 the city again suffered severely from famine. It was now under the emperor's subhedar at Haidarabad; and, when the Nizam-ul-Mulk proclaimed his independence in 1724, it became part of his possessions. In 1760 it was ceded to the Peshwa. During the period it was under the Marathas the city suffered severely. They found in its public buildings a mine of material which they immediately proceeded to appropriate. The palaces were stripped of all their wood-work; beams, doors, and windows were ruthlessly torn out and carted away; and so, when we look upon the remains of these old buildings to-day, the ravaging hand of man upon them is painfully apparent, beside which the disintegrating process of time is nothing. Famines visited the now forlorn city at frequent intervals and still further decimated its population. Many families left it and took up their abode in distant towns where their descendants still live. A few of the leading families remained behind, and their representatives are now almost in poverty. In 1818 it passed into the hands of the Raja of Satara, and, later on, Bijapur, together with the rest of the Satara kingdom, reverted to the British. It was for some time part of the Satara Collectorate, then it was handed over to Sholapur, and finally became a *taluka* of the Kaladgi district. Lately Kaladgi was given up as the head-quarter station and Bijapur was selected as such. It is now the chief town of the Bijapur Collectorate of the Bombay Presidency, and at it reside the Collector, Judge, and other officers in charge of that district.

FARES OF PUBLIC CONVEYANCES.

(ABSTRACT.)

For Town Tongas, Bullock Shigrams or Dummies, and Labour Carts for luggage and goods.	Victoria, Tonga, Dogcart, Buggy, or other two-wheeled horsed Carriage.		Shigram or Dummies, with a pair of bullocks or ponies.		For Labour Carts to carry luggage and goods.	
	Rs.	AS.	Rs.	AS.	Rs.	AS.
Engaged by hour.						
For the first hour	0	8	0	12	0	0
Over each subsequent hour or broken period over the hour	0	4	0	6	0	0
Whole day commencing from an hour after sunrise to 7 p.m.	2	0	2	0	0	0
From 7 p.m. to midnight	1	8	1	8	0	0
If detained after midnight, additional	1	0	1	0	0	0
Engaged by distance.						
From any gentleman's bungalow to the Railway station	0	8	0	8	0	8
Vice versa	0	8	0	8	0	8
Round the station and back to Bungalow within three hours	1	0	1	0	0	0

N.B.—Owners of Tongas and Carts, etc., can accept less but may not ask for more than the above rates.

Every driver must have with him the authorised rates of fares, together with an abstract of the laws relating to Public Conveyances, which he must produce, if demanded by a passenger.

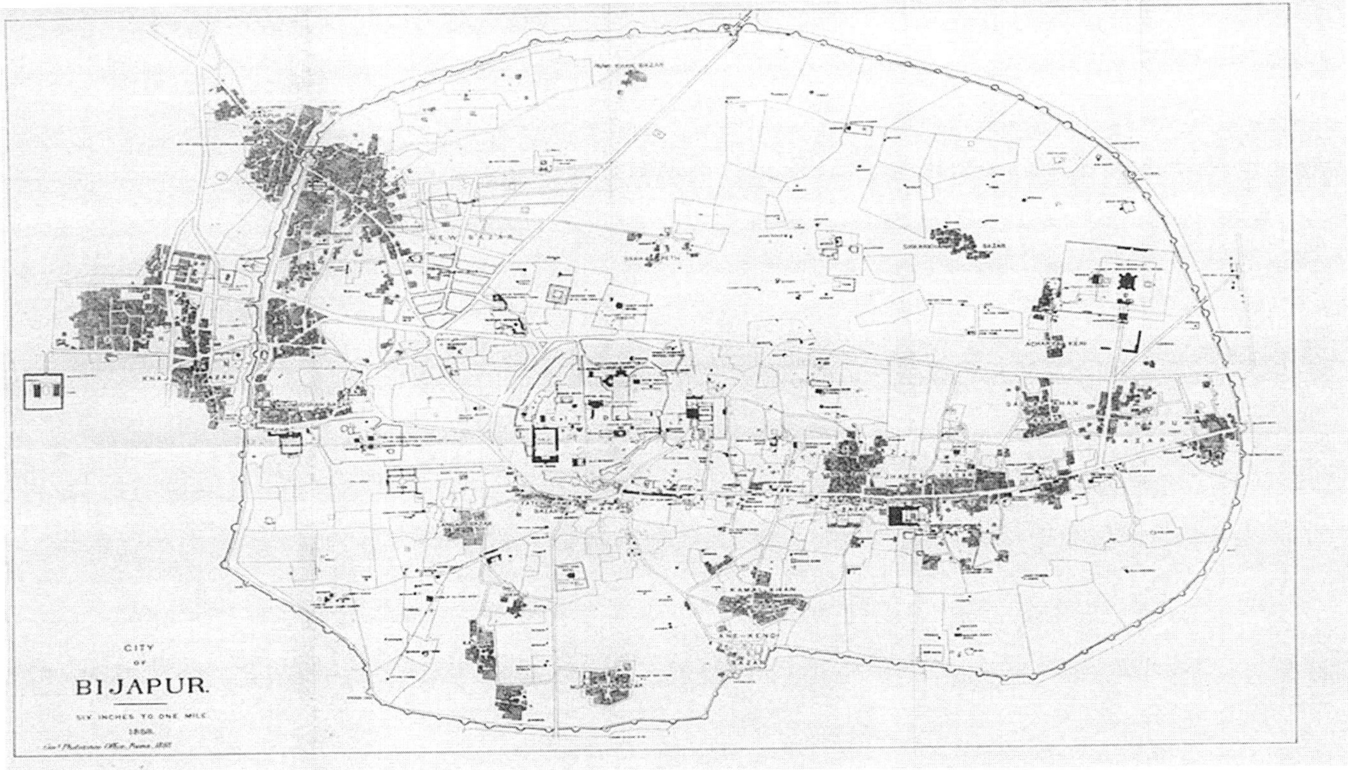
CITY
OF
BIJAPUR.
SIX INCHES TO ONE MILE.
NEW BAZAR

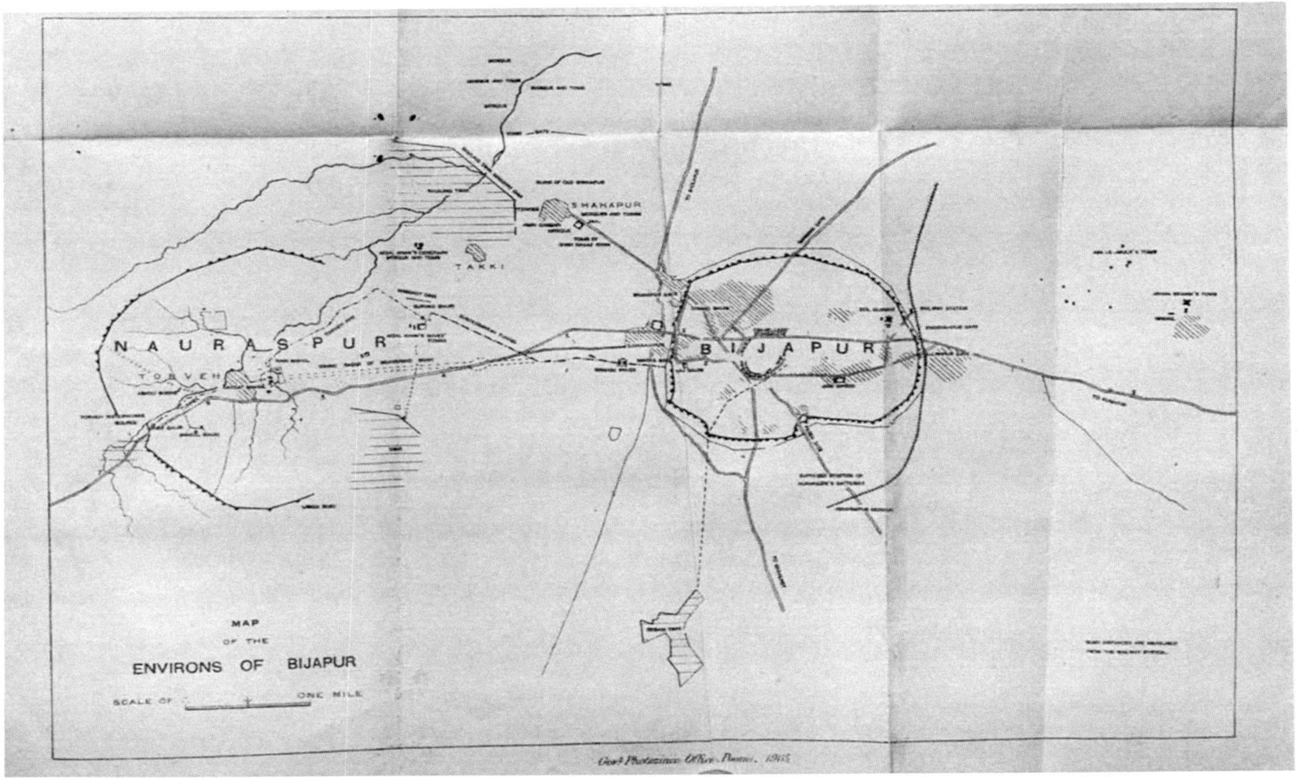

MAP
OF THE
ENVIRONS OF BIJAPUR
SCALE OF ONE MILE
NAURASPUR
TORVEH
TAKKI
SHAHAPUR
BIJAPUR
Govt Photozinco Office, Poona.